Life Stories

A Study In
Christian Decision
Making

Jo Perry-Sumwalt
and
John Sumwalt

CSS Publishing Company, Inc.
Lima, Ohio

BV4501.2
.S847
1995

Scripture passages unless marked are from the *New Revised Standard Version of the Bible,* copyright 1989, by the Division of Christian Education of the National Council of the Churches of Christ in the USA. Used by permission.

Scripture passages marked KJV are from the *King James Version of the Bible,* in the public domain.

Library of Congress Cataloging-in-Publication Data

Sumwalt, John E.
    Life stories : a study in Christian decision making / John Sumwalt and Jo Perry-Sumwalt.
        p.   cm.
    Includes bibliographical references.
    ISBN 0-7880-0330-5
    1. Christian life. 2. Decision-making — Religious aspects — Christianity. I. Perry-Sumwalt, Jo. 1952- II. Title.
BV4501.2.S847   1995
248.4—dc20   94-35603
                                                  CIP

ISBN: 0-7880-0330-5   PRINTED IN U.S.A.

*For our parents, Phyllis and Lester Perry,
Bernice and Leonard Sumwalt.*

*And to Kim Stout, Kerri Sherwood, Frank Gaylord,
Cynthia Connor, Clarice Kratz, Ken Anderson,
and Paul Ketterer, friends in time of need.*

Contents

Introduction

Jesus, and other Jewish rabbis before and after him, gave moral instruction by telling parables and retelling old stories to address the issues of their day. We still live by many of these old stories. We call them scripture. They help us to understand who and whose we are; they help us decide what is right and what is wrong: what is loving and good for our lives. We would be lost without the parables Jesus told and the stories in the Old Testament. When we have important moral and ethical decisions to make, we remember how the characters in these stories acted in difficult situations. Their stories make it possible for us to learn from them as surely as if they were with us in the flesh.

The new stories which we have created for this study reinterpret some of these old stories in ways that address the new ethical and moral problems we face today. It is an old, tried and true way of decision making.

How should we treat the aged and how can we prepare ourselves for old age? Should the church forbid divorce in all circumstances? What can we do to help the homeless? Can drunk drivers be forgiven?

Let us tell you a story.

Chapter 1

Flesh

---

*And the word became flesh and lived among us, and
we have seen his glory . . .*

John 1:14a

Uncle Patrick came to live with us after Gram died, in the
fall of my senior year. I had hoped that the big room behind
the stairs, with its convenient outside entrance, would be mine,
but Mom said I would have to wait. Uncle Patty, as we all
called him, needed a place to live. He was her only brother
and my only uncle. Dad had all sisters in his family. He was
reluctant to have Uncle Patty stay with us, but Mom insisted.
"It will only be for a little while," she said, "until his disability comes through from the government." Uncle Patty was
disabled because of his weight and a chronic heart condition.
To say that he was a big man would be a gross understate-
ment. Uncle Patty was huge: six-foot-six, 580 pounds: a hulking mass of quivering, flabby flesh. The whole house quaked
and creaked whenever he moved about in his room. The mattress and springs on Gram's big four-poster bed were soon sag-
ging all the way to the floor. He used to open up his shirt and
show us kids his massive stomach. It looked like an unruly
sack of feed when he picked it up in both hands and let it spill
out over his belt. "It's all paid for," he always said. And then
he would laugh that deep, guttural, fat man's laugh that we
all came to love so dearly that year he was with us.

Mom told us that he had always been fat, even as a small
child. She said the kids at school used to taunt him with "fatty,
fatty Patty" and "Pat's so fat he can sit on his own lap." Uncle
Patty learned to shrug it off. He told me one time, during one
of our late night walks down by the river, that the first couple

of years of high school were the worst, until he came to realize that everyone is handicapped in some way. His was just more obvious than others. He said he made a conscious decision when he was 16 years old to befriend people who had been hurt as he was hurt and to try in some small way to help them feel better about themselves. That was probably why he was one of the most loved persons in town. Uncle Patty was caring and sensitive in a way that didn't draw attention to himself. People just liked him. He had a warmth about him which I now recognize, as I look back with the perspective of some years, as a healing presence. Spirits were lifted whenever he came into a room. You knew that he would say or do something that would be uplifting to everyone. I'm not trying to say that he was the life of the party; Uncle Patty in no way fit the stereotype of the jolly fat man. He was a gentle, nurturing soul, gifted with an exceptional intellect and a discerning perceptivity about the meaning of relationships and events that set him apart from most other men and women of his time. The enormity of his obese frame which repulsed most people upon first meeting, and caused children to point and stare whenever he went about in public, made no difference whatsoever to those of us who loved him. His physical ugliness was part of his glory. To me he will always be the very incarnation of grace and love.

Uncle Patty was one of the few adults I knew in my late adolescent years who treated me as an equal. He listened seriously to what I had to say. And he didn't spare my feelings if I acted foolishly or said something stupid. He always told me exactly what he thought. To this day, whenever I am in any kind of trouble or wonder what to do in a difficult situation, I ask myself, "What would Uncle Patty think about this?" And then it is almost as if I can hear his voice and see his face through the fog, just as I did when he found me that cold December night, bleeding and half dead along the river road.

I had been at a dance on the other side of town with some friends. Uncle Patty had let me drive his 1949 Chrysler Saratoga

Coupe — the silver anniversary model. Oh, what a car that was! Uncle bought it used from the Fuller Brush man, but it was in mint condition. It had a hemi V8 engine, an hydraulically operated transmission, gyrol fluid drive, hydralizer shock absorbers, and safety level ride. It could go from zero to 60 in ten seconds, and it had fold back seats. My friends were impressed.

When we arrived at the hall, one of the guys announced that he knew someone who could get us a couple of six packs. We all chipped in and after only a few minutes he came back with the beer. We drank a round before we went in to the dance, and we had a couple more each when the band took their break near the end of the evening. I had been warned about drinking and driving, but I thought a couple of beers wouldn't hurt — and it would have been awkward to turn down a drink in front of my friends. I felt fine when we started home: a little tired, but certain that my driving abilities were in no way impaired. I dropped my friends off at their homes and had made the final turn on the river road, just a half-mile from our house, when I suddenly lost control of the car. I have never been exactly sure what happened, whether I was going too fast as I came out of the curve or if I hit a slippery spot in the road. The last thing I remember was the car rolling over the embankment toward the river. I thought, this is it, and then I blacked out. They told me later that I was thrown from the car before it went into the water. I don't know how long I lay there in the snow before Uncle Patty found me. When I came to, he was kneeling over me, saying my name.

"Buzz, are you all right? Are you okay?"

"I don't know," I finally managed to say.

"Well, you're alive at least," he said with some relief in his voice. Then he wrapped me in his coat, picked me up, and carried me all the way to the house. Somehow he was able to get me into the backseat of Dad's old Studebaker without adding to my injuries. Then I must have passed out again. I woke up in the hospital bed a few hours after the surgery. Uncle Patty was there with my folks. They all seemed greatly relieved that I was alive and that I would have no permanent disabilities. Nothing was said about my drinking and driving until I was almost well enough to go home. Dad simply told me that I would have to face the music in court and would likely lose my license until I was 21. He suggested that I take the lumps I had coming and learn from it. No one said anything about the car. I knew how much Uncle Patty loved that big Chrysler. When I offered to pay it off, bit by bit, by working extra hours after school, he shook his head and said, "I'm just glad you're okay." I'll never forget that, but it was what he said and did later that left the biggest impression.

It was on Christmas day, my last day in the hospital. Uncle Patty got there about an hour before the rest of the family arrived. He said, "Buzz, you know that what you did was inexcusable. Drinking and driving is a sin against the community. You risked not only your own life, and those of your friends, but the life of everyone else who was on the road that night. You could have killed someone or several people, including yourself. The fact that you didn't makes you no less guilty than a criminal who attempts to murder someone with a gun or a knife. To drink even one drop of alcohol, or to take any other kind of drug that reduces your physical and mental abilities before driving, is inexcusable — but not unforgivable."

Then he smiled at me and said, "If we all got what we deserved, life would be unbearable. I once did exactly the same thing you did. Your dad was with me. No one ever found out about our little accident. But he remembers it as well as I do. And now he and I both are kicking ourselves because we didn't prevent you from making the same mistake. Maybe we all have to learn our own hard lessons."

I have never forgotten what he said to me that day, or what he did just before Mom and Dad and the rest of them came into the room with my Christmas presents. He leaned over the bed, put his big, flabby arms around me, drew me in close to his massive frame and hugged me with all of his might. I knew then that everything would be all right.

Story Questions

1. With whom do you identify in the story? Buzz, Uncle Patty, Dad, Mom, the taunters, Buzz's friends, (the '49 Chrysler)?

2. Thin is in. Dieting is a national obsession. There is much prejudice against obese persons in our society. What attitude do you think Christians should hold toward themselves and others who are overweight?

3. Have you ever been teased or taunted as Uncle Patty was as a child? Did you ever take part in the taunting of others?

4. Do you agree with Uncle Patty's conclusion that "... everyone is handicapped in some way"? How have you learned to cope with your own handicaps and disabilities?

5. Did you have an Uncle Patty in your life when you were a teenager — an adult who served as a role model and mentor? Are you aware of serving this function for children or teenagers in your life?

6. Do you think that Buzz's father and Uncle Patty have any responsibility for Buzz's mistake, as is suggested in the story?

7. Have you ever been tempted to drive after drinking, taking medication, or when you were sleepy? Do you agree with Uncle Patty's statement to Buzz that "Drinking and driving is a sin against the community. You risked not only your own life and those of your friends, but the life of everyone else who was on the road that night. You could have killed someone, or several people, including yourself. The fact that you didn't makes you no less guilty than a criminal who attempts to murder someone with a gun or a knife"?

13

8. Do you agree with Uncle Patty's next statement to Buzz: "To drink even one drop of alcohol, or to take any other kind of drug that reduces your physical and mental abilities before driving, is inexcusable — but not unforgivable."

9. What is the act of love in this story?

Digging Into The Text

*And the word became flesh and lived among us, and we
have seen his glory, the glory as of a father's only son,
full of grace and truth.*

From his fullness we have all received, grace upon grace.
John 1:14a, 16

You know the saying, "The spirit ... is willing, but the
flesh is weak." It is not true — at least not entirely true in
the way we have come to understand it in the twentieth century.
It is, indeed, a quote of what Jesus said to his disciples in the
garden of Gethsemane after he found them sleeping. He was
praying and struggling for his life and they were asleep. He
said to them, "Keep awake and pray that you may not come
into the time of trial: The spirit indeed is willing but the flesh
is weak" (Matthew 26:41 and Mark 14:38). We understand
what Jesus is saying to the disciples, and we know that they
fell asleep again despite his warning. But Jesus did not fall
asleep. He did not yield to the temptation to save his own life
and deny his calling. He prayed, "Father, for you all things
are possible; remove this cup from me, yet not what I want,
but what you want" (Mark 14:36). Jesus accepted the cross
— and he, too, was flesh. That is what we are tempted to deny.

An argument among early Christians over Jesus' human
and divine qualities led to a heresy called *docetism,* which held
that Jesus' body only appeared to be real, and therefore he
only seemed to suffer and die on the cross (Brauer 271). But
it did not end in the early centuries. M. Scott Peck suggests
in his book, *The Different Drum,* that a vast majority of
church-going American Christians are also heretics, because
they practice what he calls "pseudodocetism." Peck explains
that most American Christians have enough education through
catechism or confirmation to recognize that there is a contradiction in the claim that Jesus is both human and divine. To com-
pensate for the contradiction, they place much more value upon

15

his divinity than his humanity, putting him on God's level, 99.5% divine, and leaving us on an earthly level, 99.5% human. The gulf created by this distancing relieves ordinary human beings from responsibility for Christ-like actions (297). In Peck's words:

> *Because that gulf is so great, American Christians are not seriously encouraged to attempt to bridge it. When Jesus said all those things about being the way and that we were to take up our cross and follow him, and that we were to be like him and might even do greater things than he did, he couldn't possibly have been serious, could he? I mean, he was divine, and we're just human. So it is, through the large scale ignoring of Jesus' very real humanity, that we are allowed to worship him in name without the obligation of following in his footsteps. Pseudodocetism lets us off the hook (297-8).*

Human beings are reluctant to take on the burdens we so proudly praise Jesus for bearing. We claim to be less because of his divinity . . . weaker because of our humanity. Yes, we do yield to temptations of the flesh — and the body does grow feeble from illness and old age — but the flesh is not weak. If you doubt this, put your little finger in a baby's hand and feel the strength in that grip. The flesh is strong. And it is in flesh that we know the power of the almighty God.

"The word became flesh and lived among us . . . ." God became known to us in the body of a human being like ourselves. He was born, he breathed, he nursed, he slept, he woke, he cried (it was three o'clock in the morning. Joseph poked Mary, "Honey, the baby's crying. I think he needs you." And Mary got up and changed his swaddling clothes), and he laughed as we do. He grew in stature and in wisdom, he worked, he played, he loved, he grieved, he suffered, and he died. And his dead flesh was raised up alive from the grave; not just his spirit or his soul, his flesh — his whole body — was resurrected. Jesus said to Thomas, who doubted that he was really present in the flesh, "Put your finger here and see my hands. Reach out your hand and put it in my side.

Do not doubt but believe." Thomas answered him, "My Lord and my God!" (John 20:27, 28). Thomas was convinced of the resurrection when he saw and touched the wounds in Jesus' flesh. "Jesus said to him, "Have you believed because you have seen me? Blessed are those who have not seen and yet have come to believe" (John 20:29).

Many of us who follow Jesus are like Thomas before he saw and touched. We cannot believe that Jesus is alive in both body and spirit. We know him as spirit, but his flesh is not real to us. And since, unlike Thomas, we have had no opportunity (or have not taken an opportunity) to see and touch, we cannot be counted among those Jesus called "blessed." We want to believe, but we cannot let go of the dualist traditions which have crept into our ideas and rituals. "Ashes to ashes and dust to dust," we say. "The body we commit to the ground, to its resting place, but the spirit we commend to God." It is not so. Neither the Hebrew scriptures nor the New Testament makes any such distinction. Body and soul, flesh and spirit, are not separate entities. We are one.

James Lynwood Walker writes in his book *Body and Soul*, that we need to understand the ancient Israelitic word "nephesh" (soul; being) to understand the concept of the human being as a soul in totality rather than as a body supplied with a soul. These ancient people saw a relationship of complete unity between body and soul (nephesh) ... a unity of all aspects of human nature into one whole. Our own culture has been influenced by the Greek-Hellenistic dualism which overwhelmed Judeo-Christian religion in its early centuries. This dualism separates the realm of matter, considered unreal and/or evil, from a vaguely defined "spiritual" realm. It allows us to believe that no matter how terrible life may appear, there is a place "out there" where everything will be all right (36, 44). Walker sums up:

> *This dualism, which overwhelmed the Judeo-Christian religion in the early centuries of its history, has been and is a tenacious influence in this culture. Based on its influence, the Judeo-Christian religion inaugurated a split*

between body and soul which resulted in denigration, if not outright condemnation, of the body. As a carrier of the instincts, the body was labeled despicable and sinful (44).

Sinful though it may be, flesh is part of our essence. The Lord God formed it from the dust of the ground and breathed into it the breath of life, and we became living beings. Flesh (Genesis 2:7, paraphrase). The word became flesh, lived flesh, died flesh, rose ... flesh!

"And we have seen his glory ...." What does it mean to say that we have seen Jesus' glory? Have you ever seen someone's glory?

I looked in on the kindergarten Sunday school class one day, and there was Eleanor Kemp, one of the retired members of our congregation, leaning over the table with the little children huddled all around her, light shining in their eyes, listening intently to her every word. She and the children were in their glory.

When we see Jesus in the scripture with the children on his knee, when we see him healing the sick, feeding the hungry, eating with a sinner, touching a leper, angry in the temple, weeping at a grave, breaking bread with the disciples, standing trial before Pilate, being whipped and crucified, dying on the cross, and resurrected from the grave, we see his glory, "... glory as of a father's only son, full of grace and truth ..." (John 1:14).

"From his fullness," John says, "we have all received grace upon grace" (1:16).

Grace comes to us in the flesh. Forgiveness, mercy, pardon, love, and healing are administered through living beings: in a voice, in an embrace, in a kiss, in a touch, in the flesh. Someone forgives you and gives you another chance when you don't deserve it; someone picks you up when you fall; someone touches you where you hurt, and you are healed. "Mommy, kiss it and make it better," we say, "best medicine in the world." The word becomes flesh again and again and again ....

Digging Into The Text Questions

1. Do you agree with M. Scott Peck's statement that we have more faith in the divinity of Jesus than in his humanity? Does this belief prevent us from practicing his teachings?

2. What do you think it means to say we have seen Jesus' "glory"? Have you ever seen someone's glory? (Glory referred to the revealing nature of God which was sometimes apparent in a physical radiance. See the account of Moses' shining face in Exodus 24:15-17 and 34:29-35. Also see Psalm 85:9-10 and the accounts of Jesus' transfiguration in Matthew 17:1-8, Mark 9:2-8, and Luke 9:29-36.)

3. The Gnostics taught that the higher knowledge of God was revealed to only a few spiritual, elite Christians. John responds to this heresy emphatically in verse 16 saying: "And from his fullness we have *all* received grace upon grace." How have you experienced grace in your life? Can you say that you have known God in the flesh?

Works Cited

Brauer, Jerald C. et al. "Docetism." *The Westminster Dictionary of Church History*. Philadelphia: Westminster Press, 1971.

Peck, M. Scott. *The Different Drum*. New York: Simon & Schuster, 1987.

Walker, James Lynwood, *Body and Soul: Gestalt Therapy and Religious Experience*. Nashville: Abingdon, 1971.

Chapter 2

Where Could I Carry My Shame?

... he took hold of her, and said to her, "Come, lie with me, my sister." She answered him, "No, my brother, do not force me; for such a thing is not done in Israel; do not do anything so vile! As for me, where could I carry my shame?"

2 Samuel 13:11b-13a

At first Valerie felt numb, and the activity around her seemed like a nightmare — unreal. Lifted and carried like a broken doll, sped through the night accompanied by multi-colored flashes of light and a never-ending wail of sirens, she watched the events unfolding around her as if she were watching a documentary on television, but the images and sounds were distorted and distant. Then people began touching her and there was pain. She panicked and lashed out, but there were too many of them, and she was already too weak to fight. Strangers came and went, faces loomed over her. She was medicated, swabbed, x-rayed, stitched, and bandaged, but always aware that someone was there with a camera, snapping pictures, blinding her with repeated flashes. She didn't break down until Margaret stepped up to her bedside. Then the numbness in her mind and the pain in her body gave way to the humiliation of her spirit. Margaret was her best friend at work, but Valerie knew that she wasn't paying a social call. Margaret was there to counsel her, because Valerie had just been raped.

"Are you still in pain?" Margaret asked as tears made their way down the swollen bruises and bandaged cuts on Valerie's face. The only answer was a slight shake of her head.

"I'm a real mess," Valerie tried to say, but the words came out thick and distorted and she realized that her jaw had been wired. When she raised her eyes from the IV needle taped to her left arm to look at Margaret's face, she saw that a police officer was waiting by the door with a pad and pencil. She braced herself for the questions she had to answer.

There really wasn't a lot to tell. Valerie knew the man — the attendant at the Bridge Street parking ramp where she always parked her car. She had said good morning to him every day for several weeks. Today another man had worked the morning shift and the attendant she knew had been on duty when she came out to the ramp after working late. She had walked with another co-worker past the booth, expressed her surprise that the attendant was working nights, and made some off-hand remark about having missed him that morning. She left her friend at his car, declining the offer of a ride down one level to hers, and the friend drove away. Just after she reached her car and unlocked the door, a voice behind her asked if she had dropped a glove. When she turned to look the attendant was standing there, and he struck her in the face with his fist, pushed her into the front seat, and drove to the top level of the ramp where he beat and raped her inside the car.

The policeman thanked her for her cooperation and took the information and the name and description of the attendant, promising to try for a swift arrest.

"You do plan to press charges, don't you, ma'am?" the officer said. Valerie felt very much exposed and vulnerable. She had counselled enough rape victims to know what going to trial meant for a woman already traumatized by rape. Everything would have to be told again and again. The judge and jury would be shown the pictures the police photographer had been snapping of her throughout her examination and treatment. Everyone involved would know just what he had done to her. Her shame, if not her name, would be made public. But even as the horror of what she would be forced to endure flashed through her mind, the professional in Valerie acknowledged that she must press charges to get the rapist off the streets, and she nodded her assent. The officer left and Margaret sat quietly with her until the sedative put her to sleep.

In two days' time the bruises and cuts began to heal and Valerie was released from the hospital. Margaret took her home to her apartment, but Valerie felt uneasy and insecure there. They had talked daily, Margaret doing her job of counselling in a more intimate, personal manner than either of them used at work. But Valerie's feelings of humiliation had been replaced by a growing sense of rage and injustice, and the terrible fear that it could all happen again at any time haunted her. Margaret warily noted the daily changes to Valerie's apartment as well as the signs that her friend was beginning to shut out all of the outside world. First there were two new locks on the front door. Then, even though the apartment was on the third floor, Valerie had iron bars installed on the three windows that faced the alleyway. Whenever Margaret called, the answering machine would pick up on the second ring, and Valerie would only answer when she knew who the caller was and what he or she wanted. Valerie was often out of groceries and other necessities because she wouldn't go out for them herself and she refused to ask for help. When Margaret confronted her about her growing isolation, Valerie finally broke down and cried.

"I'm sorry, Margaret! I don't mean to shut you out, but I feel so vulnerable. It's like I've lost the ability to trust. I can't even make myself go down to get the mail from my mailbox because I'm afraid someone will grab me. I can't look any man in the eye, because any man could do to me what he did. I keep thinking it would never have happened if I had accepted Gene's offer of a ride down to my car. It's partly my fault for not being on my guard. Now I can't go anywhere or do anything because I might slip up again. It's not rational, I know that, but I can't get rid of the feeling. My training and my intellect have nothing to do with it — I hate that man so much that I honestly believe I'd torture and mutilate him if I had the chance."

"You just told me your intellect and training have nothing to do with your feelings, Val, but try, just try for a minute, to think about what you just said," Margaret said softly.

"What you're going through is perfectly normal and natural. You have a right to feel outraged. That man not only degraded you, he stole your sense of security from you. But don't let the feelings carry you away. Get a hold of reality. Talk with your pastor or a psychologist. If what I'm doing isn't helping you, get more help! Just don't let this anger and fear become an obsession that ruins your life."

" 'He' ruined my life!" Valerie said sharply.

"No!" Margaret said just as sharply. "He hurt you for no reason and he frightened you, but your reaction is what's ruining your life. Let go of the hate! You can't recover until you let go!"

Valerie sat and considered what her friend had said long after Margaret had gone. It was Thursday, 12 days since the rape, and except for the wire holding her broken jaw in place and fading bruises and cuts, her body had recovered from the attack. Her life, she now realized, had not. On Monday she was scheduled to go back to work — to face and attempt to counsel other women who were feeling exactly what she now felt. How could she do that when the rage inside her was still so strong? How could she encourage other women to step past that rage when she had not? How could she possibly let go and move on?

When the telephone rang she was startled out of her thoughts and surprised to find herself in the dark. She had been totally unaware that the afternoon had passed. Valerie listened as the taped message announced to the caller that she couldn't come to the phone, but reached out instinctively to answer when she heard the police officer's voice say they had good news for her.

"We arrested the suspect this afternoon when he tried to pick up his last paycheck at work," the officer said. "We'll need you to identify him in a line-up. Could you come down tomorrow morning?"

After Valerie had put down the phone she realized that her hand was shaking and she was wet with sweat. She had agreed to identify her rapist, but she knew that she was not prepared

24

to look at him. She picked up the phone again and called Margaret with the news, and to arrange for her friend to accompany her to the police station. Then, with some difficulty, she dialed the number of her church and made an appointment to see the pastor. When she tried to contact Margaret again, Margaret was out, and Valerie had to face making it to, and through, the appointment alone.

It seemed strange to Valerie to be outside after dark, even though it has been less than two weeks since the attack. The police had returned her car, which had been dusted for fingerprints and tested for blood and semen samples. She tried not to look at the bloodstains on the light blue upholstery of the passenger's side of the front seat, where her head had been. Even though she had checked both the trunk and the back seat before she got into the car, she couldn't help darting glances into the rearview mirror as she drove the seven blocks to the church. She could see through the office window that the pastor was on the phone when she arrived, and knowing she was nearly 15 minutes early, Valerie paced the narthex, listening with some interest to a deep alto voice crooning old-time spirituals somewhere in the building. When her pacing took her past the sanctuary doors, she could see that the voice belonged to Mrs. Harris, the church custodian, who was dusting the pews. Valerie opened the sanctuary door quietly and took a seat in the back pew.

The darkness and shifting shadows around her made Valerie feel uneasy. But the strong, steady voice was comforting, and soon her mind focused on the words of the songs as well as the sound of the voice:

> *There is a balm in Gilead to make the wounded whole.*
> *There is a balm in Gilead to heal the sinsick soul.*
> *Sometimes I feel discouraged, and think my work's in*
>   *vain,*
> *But then the holy spirit revives my soul again.*
> *Don't ever feel discouraged, for Jesus is your friend,*
> *And if you look for knowledge he'll ne'er refuse to lend.*

Valerie found the words as soothing as the voice, and rose, while the old woman's back was turned, to announce her presence and avoid startling her.

"Good evening, Mrs. Harris," she called from the doorway.

The custodian turned toward the voice and squinted into the gloom at the back of the sanctuary.

"Good evening. I'm afraid my old eyes can't make you out in the shadows."

"It's Valerie Mason," she said, stepping forward into the light. "I was just waiting to see Pastor Avery and I heard you singing. I wanted to tell you how warm and comforting your songs are to me tonight."

The older woman smiled as Valerie approached, and stretched out her right hand in greeting. Valerie shook it.

"Those old gospel songs have seen me through years of pain and pleasure. I hardly even know I'm singing them anymore, they're such a part of me."

"Well, they've touched me tonight, when I needed to hear them, and I thank you."

The custodian's eyes searched Valerie's face for a moment, then her countenance softened and her hand, still clasping the younger woman's in greeting, tightened briefly: an almost imperceptible squeeze.

"He hurt you bad, didn't he?" she asked, out of nowhere, and Valerie's eyes widened in surprise. There had been no preliminary questions as to her fading bruises and abrasions. The older woman had made no comment on her muffled voice and asked nothing about how she had been hurt, and there was no way she could have known. Valerie's name, according to the law, had not been disclosed in the news reports of the rape. Yet Valerie know instinctively that Mrs. Harris understood exactly what she had been through.

"How did you know?" she asked when she finally found her voice.

"I recognized it in your eyes, child. It's the same look I saw whenever I looked in the mirror over many, many years."

26

Valerie was stunned, partly because it had never occurred to her that anyone could read her experience in her face, but mostly because of what Mrs. Harris had just shared with her about her own life.

"Someone hurt you this way, too?" she asked in a voice so soft it was almost inaudible.

"Even worse, for me, it was someone I loved," the old woman nodded.

Valerie had to sit down, and Mrs. Harris joined her in the pew. "Was it someone in your family?" she managed to ask. Although the questions in her mind corresponded with her training, they had nothing to do, at this time, with counselling.

"My father," the old voice affirmed, and Valerie searched the old woman's dark eyes for some trace of the pain, the anguish, the shame she knew was visible in her own. They were not there. The sadness Mrs. Harris experienced from bringing up the old memories was accompanied only by her normal, placid disposition.

Although she tried to hold them back, the tears spilled over her eyelids as Valerie asked the next question. "Will it take a long, long time for the anger and the fear to go away?"

"It can," Mrs. Harris answered carefully, "depending on how long it takes you to be able to forgive."

Valerie recoiled as if she'd been slapped. "Forgive?" The idea of putting the experience behind her and getting on with her life had been working its way through Valerie's mind, but forgiveness had never occurred to her. How could she ever forgive that stranger for the things he had done to her — for all he had taken away from her in a single, brutal action?

"I know, it's not even a possibility in your mind as yet, but remember, child, I'm speaking to you after years and years of hating and hurting. There does come a time, when your heart is weary of hating, and your soul aches to stop the hurting, that your mind realizes you have to let go. Your hurt is new, and your hatred is still strong, but believe me, Miss Mason, if your mind allows you to let go, the hurting stops. It's not possible for me to tell you to forgive him. I have never forgiven my father for what he stole from me, because he never told me, in all of the rest of his life, that he was truly sorry. To forgive him when he wasn't sorry would be like saying it was okay for him to do what he did. But I have forgiven his sickness: his weakness. That way I could let go of my hate and live again. When you see that wretched man who hurt you in all of his sickness and sin, and let go of your anger, it will help you live again.''

When Pastor Avery stepped into the sanctuary to invite Valerie into his office, and saw the young woman weeping on Mrs. Harris' shoulder, he knew his job had just been made easier.

The following morning, when Margaret accompanied Valerie to the police station for the line-up, she could feel a change in her friend. Valerie was nervous, even frightened, but there was an intangible difference in her attitude that puzzled Margaret. Valerie held tightly to her friend's hand while they waited in semi-darkness for the group of suspects to be lined up behind the glass wall of an illuminated, adjoining room. They had both experienced this procedure many times before with clients. Margaret prepared herself for Valerie's tension and anxiety to be released in any number of ways — anger, tears, cursing, rage — yet was totally unprepared for what actually happened.

Valerie gripped her friend's hand more tightly as the first of the suspects stepped through the door of the brightly lighted room before her. The parking attendant was the third to enter. In her nervous state, she had been uncertain how she would feel when she saw him again. It was mildly surprising to her that her first impression was that he looked tired. While the police officer next to her ordered the men to face right, rear, left, and front, Valerie studied her rapist. The others were unimportant. She looked at his face carefully, unable to identify any of the rage or animosity now that she had seen in it as it hovered close over her own. Instead she saw a cold, tight-lipped, cocky assurance, and she knew that he knew she was looking at him. She looked at his large hands, with grease permanently embedded beneath the fingernails and around the cuticles. They clenched and unclenched at his sides now, powerless, but she could still see them as hard fists that smashed into her face repeatedly, and feel them ripping at her clothes, touching her. She shuddered involuntarily and fought back a wave of nausea.

"Can you identify any of these men as the perpetrator, Miss Mason?" the police officer asked.

"He's the third man from the right," she answered with no hesitation, and to Margaret's surprise, no emotion.

"Are you certain?"

"Yes, I'm sure it's him. That's the man who raped me."

Margaret looked at her, puzzled, as the police officer dismissed the suspects. "Val, are you all right?"

"Yes ... and no. Everything he did to me came back exactly the way it happened while I was looking at him, and I felt sick. Just seeing him brought back every detail of the attack. But, at the same time, he was just this guy from the parking garage, standing there with dirty fingernails. I hate him for what he did to me, and I want him to be locked away where he can't hurt other women, but this wasn't what I expected. I expected to see a monster, and all I saw was a man."

Margaret smiled. "Good for you, kid. I think you've just begun to let go."

Valerie shook her head. "I don't know. There's a lot of hate and fear inside of me that I haven't even touched yet. Right now I feel kind of numb, but I get nauseous when I think of having to tell what he did to me in court — and of his defense attorney trying to turn things around to make me seem to blame. I know it will happen and it makes me want to scream. Then I think of all the women and girls I've urged to endure their testimony in court, to get their lives back, I said. I don't know what I'll feel later, but I know I can't keep hiding out. I want *my* life back. I don't want to be a victim anymore."

Story Questions

1. Do you think it was right of Valerie to consider herself partly at fault for her rape? Is it fair for women to be put into the position of having to be on their guard every moment to protect themselves from rape?

2. Is it possible that a person's actions, manner of dress and body language can invite rape?

3. Why do you think Valerie feared going to court? Do you believe the criminal justice system is fair to rape victims?

4. Do you agree with Margaret that Valerie's reaction to the rape was what was ruining her life, not the rapist himself?

5. Do you agree with Mrs. Harris that forgiveness is a factor in surviving rape? Is it possible to forgive such a personal injury as rape?

6. What do you perceive as the difference between a rape victim and a rape survivor?

Permission to copy study questions for local church use granted by CSS Publishing Company, Lima, Ohio.

Digging Into The Text

David's son Absalom had a beautiful sister whose name was Tamar; and David's son Amnon fell in love with her. Amnon was so tormented that he made himself ill because of his sister Tamar, for she was a virgin and it seemed impossible to Amnon to do anything to her. But Amnon had a friend whose name was Jonadab, the son of David's brother Shimeah; and Jonadab was a very crafty man. He said to him ". . . pretend to be ill; and when your father comes to see you, say to him, 'Let my sister Tamar come and give me something to eat, and prepare the food in my sight, so that I may see it and eat it from her hand.' " So Amnon lay down, and pretended to be ill; and when the king came to see him, Amnon said to the king, "Please let my sister Tamar come and make a couple of cakes in my sight, so that I may eat from her hand."

Then David sent . . . Tamar . . . She took dough, kneaded it, and made cakes in his sight . . . Amnon said, "Send out every one from me." So every one went out from him. Then Amnon said to Tamar, "Bring the food into the chamber, so that I may eat from your hand." So Tamar took the cakes she had made, and brought them into the chamber to Amnon her brother. But . . . he took hold of her, and said to her, "Come, lie with me, my sister." She answered him, "No, my brother, do not force me; for such a thing is not done in Israel; do not do anything so vile. As for me, where could I carry my shame? . . . I beg you, speak to the king; for he will not withhold me from you." But he would not listen to her; and being stronger than she, he forced her, and lay with her.

Then Amnon was seized with a very great loathing for her; indeed, his loathing was even greater than the lust he had felt for her. Amnon said to her, "Get out!" But she said to him, "No, my brother; for this wrong in sending me away is greater than the other that you did to me." But he would not listen to her. He called the

31

young man who served him and said, "Put this woman
out of my presence, and bolt the door after her." . . .
So his servant put her out, and bolted the door after her.
But Tamar put ashes on her head, and tore the long robe
that she was wearing; she put her hand on her head, and
went away, crying aloud as she went.

Her brother Absalom said to her, "Has Amnon your
brother been with you? Be quiet for now, my sister; he
is your brother; do not take this to heart." So Tamar
remained, a desolate woman, in her brother Absalom's
house. 2 Samuel 13:1-20

No one is immune from rape. It can happen anywhere, at
any time, in any circumstance. The victim may be very young
or very old, male or female, alone or in a group. The rapist
may be a stranger or a friend, a spouse or a date, an acquaintance or a close relative. The one common factor in rape is
that the victim ceases to be a person in the eyes of the rapist
and becomes instead an object through which anger, hatred,
rage and vengeance are vented. In the story of the rape of Tamar in 2 Samuel, there are special relational circumstances at
play. Amnon, King David's eldest son and heir to the throne,
has become obsessed with desire for his half-sister, Tamar. The
text states that ". . . he made himself ill because of his sister
Tamar; for she was a virgin, and it seemed impossible to Amnon to do anything to her" (v. 2). Tamar is a full sister to
Absalom, second in line to the throne. Many possible conflicts
of relationship could easily exist between these two half-
brothers because of their birth order, including envy and am-
bition on Absalom's part and jealousy and distrust on Amnon's. Amnon's attraction to Tamar would only serve to
complicate matters, and a relationship with her could only lead
to trouble. Yet Amnon's lust might have come to nothing if
it had not been for his crafty cousin, Jonadab, son of David's
brother Shimeah, who supplies him with a plan for rape, including the king's assistance.

Jonadab knows well all of the inner workings of the royal
family, and appears to use his knowledge to pit them against

one another. Neither of the instances in which he is mentioned in this chapter casts Jonadab in the light of a trustworthy man. He knows that Amnon, as heir, is special in his father's eyes, and that his reported illness will bring the king to him. He also knows how fragile the relationship between Absalom and Amnon is. It is Jonadab who plants the seed of the rape plan in Amnon's mind; simply play sick, request that the king send Tamar to cook something special and feed him by hand in his sickbed, and when she is close . . . . No more is even implied. And Amnon needs no further suggestions. Jonadab has set the king's daughter up to be the victim of Amnon's lust and the cause of civil strife in the kingdom. King David plays into the plan, just as Jonadab had known he would, by sending Tamar to her doom.

Tamar is not portrayed as helpless or lacking in common sense in this story. One cannot help but imagine that she is aware of Amnon's feelings for her, and has become suspicious of the circumstances of her visit to his home long before Amnon sends his servants away, leaving them alone. When her not-so-sick half-brother grabs hold of her and makes his indecent proposal, "Come, lie with me, my sister" (v. 11b), Tamar does not become hysterical. She uses a logical argument against his actions, reminding him of religious law, social opinion of such behavior, and, last of all, the effect it will have on her: ". . . where could I carry my shame?" (v. 13). She even has the presence of mind to remind him that, as his father's heir, there is nothing their father would withhold from him, including herself, if he just asks. Although David could use her marriage to a rich or royal family to forge political alliances, she has no doubt that he would give up the opportunity to please his heir (Newsom, Ringe 94). But Tamar's arguments are futile. Amnon is not interested in law, social opinion, marriage, or what becomes of his victim. He rapes Tamar, then immediately hates her even more than he had desired her.

Amnon's instant hatred of his victim is said to be a realistic reaction for one who forces dominance on another. Rapists and sadists who use such tactics are believed to be fighting what they perceive as a weakness in themselves. Their victim's defeat reminds them of their own weakness, consequently enraging them (94). Amnon's banishment of Tamar from his house redoubles the insult of her rape. Tamar has assumed, wrongly, that Amnon's lust for her meant he would want her permanently. It is bad for her that he insisted on sex with her against her will, but she thinks he will at least marry her. Amnon has no such intention. His rape of Tamar has satisfied his lust and perhaps his need to insult Absalom as well. Although she cautions him ". . . this wrong in sending me away is greater than the other which you did to me" (v. 16b), he further degrades her by having his servant throw her out of his house into the street, and she walks home, wailing and rending her garments as one in mourning. Tamar, property of the king, is now damaged property. She is no longer marriageable, has no value, no security, and no hope for happiness.

Sadly, Tamar's rape is not the worst of her abuse in this story. The King is said to be "very angry" when he hears of the incident, but *nothing* else is said of him or his actions at all, leaving the reader to believe there was no action (v. 21). Absalom's response is as cold as his heart when he advises her, "Now hold your peace, my sister; he is your brother; do not take this to heart" (v. 20b). This insult against his sister and himself is the last straw to Absalom. Although it will take him two years, his course of action is set. He will kill Amnon, whom he hates, and there is no hurry. It will happen when the time is right, when it is least expected, when Amnon has dropped his guard and is vulnerable. That his revenge of Tamar's rape is also, and perhaps mostly, a means of resolving Absalom's hatred and jealousy is only implied. But his reactions, as recorded in the scriptures, are devoid of concern for his sister and centered on himself. Betrayed by her father, used as an object of Amnon's lust, a lever of family and public upheaval for Jonadab, and a reason for murderous revenge and political advancement for Absalom, Tamar is mistreated and abandoned. The last mention of her is the chilling line, "So Tamar dwelt, a desolate woman, in her brother Absalom's house" (v. 20).

Unfortunately, desolation is still too often the plight of rape victims today. The passage of time has not altered the way some cultures and individuals view women. Recent media coverage of the Navy "Tailhook Convention" scandal (in which unknown numbers of female officers were sexually assaulted and degraded), of the mass rapes of Muslim women by Serbian soldiers in Bosnia, and of the female soldiers in Operation Desert Storm who were raped and sexually abused by their own superior officers and fellow soldiers, attests to that fact. Today one in four women will suffer rape in her lifetime. A study by the National Victim Center and the Crime Victims Research and Treatment Center of the University of North Carolina claims there were more than 683,000 women raped in 1990. And if the rapes of adolescents, male and female children, and men were included, surveyors estimate that the number of 1990 rapes would be over 1.5 million (UPI — May 4, 1992).

What many people still do not understand is that rape is not a crime of sexual need, but of the need to cause fear, pain and humiliation to the victim. It may occur as the result of an impulse or of premeditation. Anthropologist Peggy Sanday, who conducted a survey of 150 subsistence societies, found high incidences of rape to be associated with militarism, interpersonal violence in general, an ideology of male toughness and distant father-child relationships. On the other hand, rape-free societies encourage female participation in the economy and political system and male involvement in child-rearing (NYT May 16, 1989). Desolation for many victims of rape comes from their inability to move beyond the assault. Because society has long viewed the subject of sex as a taboo, and conversations about it as embarrassing, rape has become all the more a thing to hide. Although the victim may bury the event, never talk about it, perhaps even refuse to acknowledge that it happened, the trauma never goes away.

A Rockfold, Illinois, woman who was raped at 16 by a convict her father allowed to live in their home spent 12 years in terror. She paced the floor at night, repeatedly checking the locks on her doors, and sometimes even sleeping in her car for a fast getaway should her attacker return. Some peace of mind and a sense of closure to her trauma occurred when her attacker was finally found guilty of raping her and sentenced to serve 40 years in prison. Still, she reports, her anger is so great that she would like to torture him. But she hopes that the conviction, and her decision to come into the open about the rape, will serve as an explanation to those she feels have always wondered why she shakes all the time, and doesn't talk to anyone, and is so shy. She says, "I just felt like the truth would set me free" (Cohen, AP 4-12-92).

Women who survive a rape — that is those who are able to face what happened to them and go on with healthy, productive lives — will be among the first to admit that the psychological horrors of rape, the feelings of helplessness, invasion, rage, fear and grief, never completely go away. Rape victims' lives are changed forever. They relive the rape in detail, awake and asleep. They find it difficult to trust anyone, especially men, and never feel totally secure. Many are unable to go out in public alone, most go to extremes to prevent an intruder from gaining entrance into their homes, and some buy guns for protection. Some even lose their faith in God as a result of what happened to them. Rape survivor Ann Haegele, a police officer in Covington, Kentucky, said of her rapist:

> ... he raped my entire inner circle of friends and family ... my children of their mother ... my husband of his wife and companion ... my parents of a part of their daughter that can never be mended ... my friends of a trusting and secure Ann. He raped my God of an accepting and open Ann, of a forgiving and non-angry Ann.
> (Scripps Howard News Service, 9-26-92)

Some victims, like Nancy Ziegenmeyer, a rape survivor from Grinelle, Iowa, have gone public with their stories through writing books, testifying before Congress, and working toward legislation to protect women's rights. They have turned their rage toward making the public and the government aware of the plight of rape victims. Their efforts have led to legislation, and have prompted co-sponsors Senators Joseph Biden, Jr., and Barbara Boxer to re-introduce the controversial Violence Against Women Act, a bill that has previously been defeated in Congress which would make crimes such as rape and sexual assault civil rights violations. The crimes could then be prosecuted federally and women would be allowed to sue their attackers (Bender, Gannett News Service, 2-25-93). Unlike Tamar, today's women are empowering themselves so they won't have to live in desolation.

There is no redemption in the story of the rape of Tamar. David, the sinner king, is too humbled and weakened by his own sin with Uriah the Hittite and Bathsheba to punish his wayward sons Amnon and Absalom for their sins, and both of them die as a result (Little 1109). Tamar is not mentioned again. She remains, for all time, only a desolate woman. The story is a true tragedy. But women today have rape crisis counsellors, support groups, and the advantage of growing public awareness to aid them in recovery. Society as a whole can look forward to a day when women no longer have to worry about where they can carry their shame, because the shame will be considered the rapist's, not the victim's.

Digging Into The Text Questions

1. What aspects of society in Tamar's time contributed to her suffering after her rape? What similarities do women still encounter today?

2. Of the four men in the story of Tamar's rape — Amnon, Jonadab, King David and Absalom — was any one less at fault than the others? Support your answer with examples.

3. In what ways has our society improved the security of women from rape?

4. Is there any instance in which a woman should be blamed in a rape? Why or why not?

5. Consider each of the following scenarios. If you are part of a group, divide the members and give each group one question to discuss:

> 1. A 20-year-old woman returning to her apartment from the swimming pool wearing a thong bikini and towel is attacked in the hallway, pulled into a stairwell and raped. What do you think was the rapist's motive?

> 2. An 84-year-old woman, wearing a house dress and slippers, is attacked in the laundry room of her apartment building as she folds clothes, and raped. What do you think was the rapist's motive?

When you have carefully considered the questions, or when your two groups have come back together and shared their conclusions, consider the fact that the rapist in both instances was the same man. Does this change your conclusions in any way? Why or why not?

On your own, or as a whole group, consider this scenario:

3. After a loss in a particularly gruelling high school football game with their conference archrivals, several players angrily taunt the team's wide receiver who, having had a very bad game, fumbled three pass receptions, any one of which could have meant the conference victory for the team. The taunting turns to a shoving match in the shower and several tackles overpower the receiver and pin him to the floor while another player suggests that if the receiver plays like a girl, maybe he'd like being treated like one. The entire team crowds around chanting "girl, girl, girl," while two team members sodomize the receiver with a broom handle. What do you think was the rapists' motivation? Is it different from the previous examples? Why or why not?

6. What can we as individuals and parents do to help bring about changes in the way society perceives women, their roles, their rights, and their treatment? How might this impact the incidence of rape?

Works Cited

Bender, Penny, Gannett News Service, *The Chicago Sun-Times,* 25, Feb. 1993: 7.

Cohen, Sharon, Associated Press, *The Kenosha News,* 12, Apr. 1992.

Haegele, Ann, Scripps Howard News Service, *The Kenosha News,* 26, Sept. 1992: 10.

Hood, Jane C., "Why Our Society Is Rape-Prone," *The New York Times* 16, May 1989.

Little, Ganse, Exegesis of 2 Samuel, *The Interpreters Bible,* Nashville: Abingdon Press, 1952, 1109.

Newsom, Carol A., and Sharon H. Ringe, Eds., "Rape, Revenge, and Revolt: The Story of Tamar" (2 Samuel 13), *The Women's Bible Commentary,* Louisville: Westminster/John Knox Press, 1992. 93-94.

UPI Wire Service, *The Kenosha News,* 4, May 1992: 23.

Chapter 3

Help For The Homeless

. . . Is not this the fast that I choose: to loose the bonds of injustice, to undo the thongs of the yoke, to let the oppressed go free, and to break every yoke? Is it not to share your bread with the hungry, and bring the homeless poor into your house . . . ?

Isaiah 58:6-7a

Mrs. Prosperous Americana was on her way to the bank one day, to check on her investments, when she came upon a homeless person sleeping on a bench along the sidewalk. She recognized her as a woman from her lodge whom they had not seen for several years. The last word they had heard was that she had lost her husband and ended up in a mental institution. Now here she was living in the street. "Oh, my," Mrs. Americana thought to herself, "I must do something to help my poor sister." Quickly he reached into her purse and took out a large, thick wallet. She opened it, took out a crisp, new $20 bill, and then ever so gently and quietly, so as not to disturb her sleeping friend, tucked it into one of the pockets of the woman's tattered coat.

Mrs. Prosperous Americana smiled as she walked away thinking to herself how good it felt to help someone in need.

Mr. Active American Churchman was driving along a dark street in the poorest section of the city, on his way to take his turn serving at the soup kitchen, when he saw the same homeless woman sitting in the doorway of an abandoned building. He recognized her as someone he had often seen going through the line at the soup kitchen. He stopped the car, rolled down the window, and asked if she would like to ride along with him. She got in the front seat and they went to the soup kitchen together, she to eat and he to serve. After the meal, he gave her a ride to a shelter where she was given a foam pad, a small pillow, and a warm blanket, and shown a spot in the middle of the floor in a large room where she could sleep next to several other homeless persons.

Mr. Active American Churchman went home to his house in a much nicer part of the city and told his wife how good it made him feel to help someone in need.

The following morning at 7:00, when the shelter closed, the homeless woman was back out on the street. She made her usual rounds in the downtown area, collecting aluminum cans and food scraps from the dumpsters behind the stores. By late afternoon she was tired, so she sat herself down to rest on a bench in the park, across from the YMCA. Just then a naive Young American Christian, on his way to the Y for his weekly swimming lesson, noticed her, and recognizing her as a child of God, sat down beside her on the bench and introduced himself. She said her name was Barbara and they began to visit. She told him a little about her life, how she had lost her family and how she had come to live on the street. The Young Christian asked her if there was anything he could do to help. "Why, yes," Barbara said. "I would appreciate it very much if you would take me home."

Naive Young American Christian didn't think to ask where home was for her. He simply offered his arm and led her up the street toward the house where he lived with his mom and dad. He told Barbara what wonderful Christians his parents were and how happy he knew they would be to welcome her into their home.

When they arrived at his house in a very nice part of the city, Young Christian introduced Barbara to his mom and dad and told them that she had come to stay with them for a while. Mrs. Prosperous Americana and Mr. Active American Churchman were completely taken aback. They didn't know what to say.

———————————

Story Questions

1. Have you ever felt moved to give a homeless person money, as Mrs. Prosperous Americana was? Did you give the money? Why or why not?

2. Mr. Active American Churchman felt good about helping in the soup kitchen and giving Barbara a ride to the shelter, but then he went home to his wife and his comfortable house. Was he right to feel good about his "charitable acts"? What more could he have done?

3. How do you think naive Young American Christian's parents responded when he brought Barbara into their home? How would you respond if you were in their place?

Digging Into The Text

*Shout out, do not hold back! Lift up your voice like a
trumpet! Announce to my people their rebellion, to the
house of Jacob their sins. Yet day after day they seek
me and delight to know my ways, as if they were a nation that practiced righteousness and did not forsake the
ordinance of their God ...*

*... Such fasting as you do today will not make your voice
heard on high ...*

*... Is not this the fast that I choose: to loose the bonds
of injustice, to undo the thongs of the yoke, to let the
oppressed go free, and to break every yoke? Is it not to
share your bread with the hungry, and bring the homeless poor into your house; when you see the naked, to
cover them, and not to hide yourself from your own kin?*
Isaiah 58:1-2b, 4b, 6-7

What is home to you? When you need to go home, where
is it that you go? In his poem "The Death of the Hired Man,"
Robert Frost tells of a homeless person who, when it comes
his time to die, goes back to the home of the farmer for whom
he has worked on and off during his declining years. The farmer is reluctant to take him in because he has never been de-
pendable, always leaving when he is needed the most. The
farmer's wife tries to soften her husband's hardness of heart,
and there follows a dialogue in which Frost gives us a defini-
tion of home that could have come straight from the mouth
of Jesus or the prophets:

*"Warren," she said, "he has come home to die:
You needn't be afraid he'll leave you this time."*

"Home," he mocked gently.

*"Yes, what else but home?
It all depends on what you mean by home.*

Of course he's nothing to us, any more
Than was the hound that came a stranger to us
Out of the woods, worn out upon the trail."

"Home is the place where, when you have to go there,
They have to take you in."

"I should have called it
Something you somehow haven't to deserve." (153-54)

However one defines home, one of the harsh realities of our time is that there are more and more people among us who do not have it. A 1989 study by the National Alliance to End Homelessness reported that, on a given night, there are 365,000 homeless persons in the United States, and that as many as 2.3 million persons are without a home for one or more nights each year. These numbers have increased dramatically in the past ten years. Patti Davis, daughter of former President Ronald Reagan, attributes the increase directly to the policies of her father's administration. She writes:

> *Before 1981, the number of homeless people in San-*
> *ta Monica was so few that their faces were well known*
> *to the rest of us living there. So were their personalities.*
> *Some you gave money to, some you didn't. Some you*
> *knew by name.*
>
> *The change was gradual. It started with rhetoric —*
> *the Reagan Administration's pledge in 1981 to cut excess*
> *from the budget. It took us a while to realize that some*
> *of that "excess" translated into human lives, discarded*
> *onto the streets. There were cuts in food stamps and in*
> *federal subsidies for low-income housing. There was the*
> *story our President told us of a man who bought oranges*
> *with food stamps and then used the change to buy vod-*
> *ka. A flagrant violation, the Chief Executive said. We*
> *should be angry at such misuse of taxpayers' money.*
>
> *We should have been angry at the story.*
>
> *The realization was slow in coming to us — the num-*
> *ber of homeless people was increasing. The federal*
> *government released its first estimates in 1984 when*

> *the Department of Housing and Urban Development ad-*
> *mitted that somewhere between 250,000 and 350,000 peo-*
> *ple were homeless (4).*

Miss Davis confesses a fear that someone might recognize her and ask her why she did not confront her father on the issue of the homeless and argue her position with him. She admits: "I would have to try to explain that I didn't know how: How do you argue with someone who states that people who are sleeping on the grates of the streets of America 'are homeless by choice'?" (5).

There are many in America who agree with Mr. Reagan. Writer L. Christopher Awalt, after two years of working with the homeless as a volunteer at the Salvation Army and a soup kitchen in Austin, Texas, concluded, "The homeless themselves are most responsible for their predicament." He says:

> *I have seen their response to troubles, and though I'd rather report otherwise, many of them seem to have chosen the lifestyles they lead. They are unwilling to do the things necessary to overcome their circumstances. They must bear the greater part of the blame for their manifold troubles ... For every person temporarily homeless, though, there are many who are chronically so. Whether because of mental illness, alcoholism, poor education, drug addiction or simple laziness, these homeless are content to remain as they are. In many cases they choose the streets. They enjoy the freedom and consider begging a minor inconvenience. They know they can always get a job for a day or two for food, cigarettes and alcohol. The sophisticated among them have learned to use the system for what it's worth and figure that a trip through the welfare line is less trouble than a steady job. In a society that has mastered dodging responsibility, these homeless prefer a life of no responsibility at all (13).*

Others among us are simply overwhelmed by the enormity of the problem. A recent *New York Times*/CBS Poll said, "... nearly six in ten Americans now say they are encountering the homeless in their own communities or on their way to work rather than encountering them only through television or reading." The poll also showed that "... 55 percent of the respondents between 18 and 29 years old [believe] that most people have become so used to seeing the homeless that they are no longer upset by the sight" (NYT A9). In a *New York Times* article based on the results of the poll, several prominent religious leaders were quoted as expressing concern that such resignation to the plight of the poor will negatively effect the nation's values in the future, not from callousness, but from a sense of powerlessness (A1). The Rev. Joan B. Campbell, executive director of the National Council of Churches, said, "The daily encounters [with the homeless] harden many of us to some degree ... You do walk past. I've often said 'What is this doing to me?' " (A1). Sister Mary Rose McGeady, president of Covenant House in New York City, shared similar thoughts:

> *The terrible agony of it all hits me constantly. Do you give money or don't you? Are you turning away the Christ who stands in front of you in rags, or are you becoming an accomplice in someone's self-destruction? (A1).*

The prophet Isaiah, writing between 538 and 520 B.C., after the return from the Babylonian exile, offers no easy escape from the ambivalence we moderns feel about helping the homeless. His admonition that the true religion, that which is most acceptable to God, "... the fast that I choose ... to share your bread with the hungry and to bring the homeless poor into your house," echoes much of what was written before him in the law and the prophets — and foreshadows what is to come from Jesus (Isaiah 59:6 & 7). Consider the following:

> *If there is among you anyone in need, a member of your community in any of your towns within the land that the Lord your God is giving you, do not be hard-hearted*

or tight-fisted toward your needy neighbor. You should rather open your hand, willingly lending enough to meet the need, whatever it may be.

(Deuteronomy 15:7-8)

This was the guilt of your sister Sodom: she and her daughters had pride, excess of food, and prosperous ease, but did not aid the poor and needy. They were haughty, and did abominable things before me; therefore I removed them when I saw it.

(Ezekiel 16:49-50)

Therefore because you trample on the poor and take from them levies of grain, you have built houses of hewn stone, but you shall not live in them; you have planted pleasant vineyards, but you shall not drink their wine.

(Amos 5:11-12)

"Come you that are blessed by my Father, inherit the kingdom prepared for you from the foundation of the world; for I was hungry and you gave me food, I was thirsty and you gave me something to drink, I was a stranger and you welcomed me, I was naked and you gave me clothing, I was sick and you took care of me, I was in prison and you visited me." Then the righteous will answer him, "Lord, when was it that we saw you hungry and gave you food, or thirsty and gave you something to drink? And when was it that we saw you a stranger and welcomed you, or naked and gave you clothing? And when was it that we saw you sick or in prison and visited you?" And the king will answer them, "Truly I tell you, just as you did it to one of the least of these who are members of my family, you did it to me." Then he will say to those at his left hand, "You that are accursed, depart from me into the eternal fire prepared for the devil and his angels; for I was hungry and you gave me no food, I was thirsty and you gave me nothing to drink, I was a stranger and you did not welcome me . . ."

(Matthew 25:34-43)

It is made plain again and again in the scriptures that there will be severe consequences for those who do not share their resources and themselves with the poor. Where there is no such sharing, there is no salvation, either personal or social. This is not to say that we are saved by our good works, but that good works, more specifically the sharing of one's life with the poor, is one sure sign of God's saving presence. Jesus says, blessed are those who care for the ". . . least of these who are members of my family" (Matthew 25:40). And Isaiah declares to the pious of his day, faithful fasting ". . . will not make your voice heard on high" (Isaiah 58:4b). If you want God to hear your prayers, ". . . bring the homeless poor into your house" (Isaiah 58:7b). This is exactly what most of us American Christians are unwilling to do. We are willing to share our food, to give clothes and money, even to give of our time working in the soup kitchens and shelters, but we refuse to bring the homeless into our homes — into our personal space — for some very good reasons.

It is risky to bring strangers into one's home. They might have an infectious disease; they might be mentally ill; they could be dangerous. Not to be cautious about such things would be irresponsible to one's self and one's family. Still, we are called to share. Isaiah and Jesus would say, figure out a way to be faithful that doesn't involve taking foolish risks. The Rev. James R. Hill of Highland, California, did just that. He says:

> *I decided that, if Jesus had a three-bedroom, two-bathroom home in the suburbs and one bedroom wasn't being used and He thought that this person probably wouldn't slit his throat at night and that he might be able to get his act together, then Jesus would invite him to come home and stay with Him for awhile. So I did.*
>
> *It grew. I have had dozens of house guests for a total of thousands of nights of lodging. I have had people with alcohol problems, drug problems, mental problems, sexual orientation problems and more. I have had folks on probation and on parole. I have had convicted felons, guys on the lam, and folks who would go on to commit*

crimes. I have had folks with athlete's foot, gonorrhea, and AIDS.

As a result, I have had more colds and more worries. I have sometimes given poorer sermons because of the load at home. I have been threatened with being fired.

Nevertheless, God has enabled me to be an agent to change lives. Many times. Some come to Christ. Some don't. Some become functioning members of society. Some don't. All are helped.

Troubled people don't just need food and shelter. They need hope. They need love, which can only be shown by long-term caring. They need reasonably healthy models of how to live. They need Christ (2).

Another good reason for not inviting the homeless into our homes is the feeling, shared by many Americans, that they don't deserve it: that, as Christopher Awalt said, they ". . . prefer a life of no responsibility" even though they have been given opportunities to make life better for themselves (Awalt 13). Isaiah and Jesus would say do it anyway. Whether they deserve our caring or not is beside the point; the homeless are children of God. In Martin Buber's book *Tales of the Hasidim: Later Masters,* there is a story titled "Interruption," which tells how one of the most respected Rabbis of the eighteenth century, learned this lesson:

One midnight when Rabbi Moshe Leib was absorbed in the mystic teachings, he heard a knock at his window. A drunken peasant stood outside and asked to be let in and given a bed for the night. For a moment the zaddik's heart was full of anger and he said to himself: "How can a drunk have the insolence to ask to be let in, and what business has he in this house!" But then he said silently in his heart: "And what business has he in God's world? But if God gets along with him, can I reject him?" He opened the door at once, and prepared a bed (85).

Our own spiritual well-being is best served when we share what we have with the homeless. God is on their side. Robert Frost's farmer was right when he defined home as ". . . the place where, when you have to go there, they have to take you in . . . ." But his farmer's wife's response to her husband is closer to the spirit of the Gospel: "I should have called it something you somehow haven't to deserve" (154).

Digging Into The Text Questions

1. Where is home to you? When you need to go home, where is it that you go, or want to go? Do you think of home in terms of people you love, a familiar place, or both? What is the most modest place that you have called home at some time in your life: a tent? a barracks? a dormitory? a mobile home? a rooming house? a small apartment? a hospital or nursing home bed? Have you ever been homeless, or feared that you might be?

2. Have you ever seen a homeless person? How many persons would you estimate are homeless in your community?

3. Do you agree with the statement that most Americans have become so used to seeing the homeless that they are no longer upset by the sight? Are we, as Christians, in danger of becoming callous to the needs of the poor because of the sense of powerlessness we feel to do anything about it, as some religious leaders have suggested?

4. Is it still true, as Isaiah declares to Israel, that "... such fasting as you do today" (pious religious practices like regular worship attendance, Bible reading, and prayer) will not make our voices heard by God?

5. Are we to understand Isaiah literally when he says to bring the homeless into our homes? Do you know anyone, like James R. Hill, who does this?

6. What are some of the root causes of homelessness in the nation and in the community where you live? How do the policies of government, large corporations, and small businesses contribute to the problems of the homeless?

7. What percentage of homeless persons do you believe are homeless by choice? Do you agree with Robert Frost's assertion in "The Death of the Hired Man" that home is "... something you somehow haven't to deserve"? Would you give aid to a homeless person who is clearly undeserving?

8. After reflecting on this passage from Isaiah, are you more likely to consider inviting a homeless person into your home?

Creative Ways To Help The Homeless

The INNS Program

The Interfaith Network of Kenosha has operated an emergency family shelter called the Shalom Center in the city for some time. When it became filled to capacity, they turned to area churches for help. The INterfaith Network Shelter, or INNS program, operates seven nights a week, alternating among seven participating church buildings. Each site has a manager and shifts of volunteers to set up the sleeping area, prepare snacks, and monitor the building from 7:00 p.m. to 7:00 a.m. Each homeless person is provided a pillow, blanket, and foam mattress for the night. The program was patterned after PADS, a homeless shelter program used in Northern Illinois.

Shelter-Pak Coats

Professor David L. Wilson, director of fashion and apparel programs at the Philadelphia College of Textiles and Science, along with students of the school and the financial backing of volunteers concerned over the welfare of thousands of Philadelphia homeless who sleep on the streets in severe weather, developed and manufactures a coat that doubles as a shelter. It is a hooded, full length, reversible coat made of wool and waterproof nylon, and designed to be as warm as a sleeping bag without zippers, buttons, or Velcro. One of the pockets is deep enough to hold the rest of the coat, which can then be worn as a backpack or used as a pillow in warmer weather. The coats weigh about 5 pounds, come in two sizes and several colors, and are distributed to the needy free of charge. Patterns and instruction kits are being made, and will be mailed free of charge to anyone who sends a written request to:

Shelter Pak
c/o Philadelphia College of Textiles and Science
42101 Henry Ave.
Philadelphia, PA 19144

For more information about the plight of the homeless in the United States, write:

National Coalition for the Homeless
Dept. P
1621 Connecticut Ave., N.W., Suite 400
Washington, D.C. 20009

The National Alliance to End Homelessness
Dept. P
1518 K St. N.W., Suite 206
Washington, D.C. 20005
Phone: 202-638-1526

Works Cited

Awalt, L. Christopher. "Brother, Don't Spare a Dime." *Newsweek*. 30 Sept. 1991: 13.

Davis, Patti. "For An Instant, She Met My Eyes." *Parade Magazine*. 23 Sept. 1990: 4-5.

deCourcy Hinds, Michael. "From Philadelphia, a Coat for the Homeless is Shelter, Too." *The New York Times*. 2, Mar. 1992: B1 + .

DiGiovanni, Joe. "Making Room at the Inn." *The Kenosha News*. 15, Dec. 1991: Section F.

Frost, Robert. "The Death of the Hired Man." *The Road Not Taken*. New York: Holt, Rinehart & Winston, 1951: 153-154.

Hill, James R. "What Would Jesus Do With Extra Bedroom?" *The United Methodist Reporter,* 23, Nov. 1991: 2.

New York Times/CBS Poll. *The New York Times*. 20, Jan. 1992: A9

Steinfels, Peter. "Apathy Is Seen Toward Agony of the Homeless." *New York Times*. 20, Jan. 1992: A1 + .

Chapter 4

Until Death Do Us Part

For this reason a man shall leave his father and mother and be joined to his wife, and the two shall become one flesh. So they are no longer two, but one flesh. Therefore, what God has joined together, let no one separate. Mark 10:7-9

Max and Irene Peters were seen together all over town for years and years: never one without the other. When they retired in the small town on the lake, they had been married for over 40 years, and Irene was in the earliest stages of Alzheimer's disease. As her confusion and disability increased, Max was devoted to her, taking over more and more of her personal care.

He took her on daily rounds of the downtown stores, shops, restaurants, and especially the Senior Citizens' Center. At first Irene could speak to answer questions and was able to feed herself if Max cut her food. Eventually he had to feed her as well as bathe her, dress her, fix her hair, and diaper her; but he never asked for help. Her moods changed from vacant silence one moment to babbling and shouting obscenities the next; and sometimes she struck out at Max when he was feeding her and knocked the spoon from his hand or the plate from the table, or fought him as he attempted to guide her on their way. He never got upset. He might scold Irene gently and tell her she mustn't cause a scene, but he never lost his temper. He'd just take her hand in his and shush her until she settled back into a docile state. Nothing came between them; they were always together.

Max began bringing Irene to Sunday services in the little community church about a year after the disease seriously affected her mind. Even there she might call out or rock and moan. Max could usually quiet her, but sometimes he had to take her out, so they always sat in the back pew, near the door. Most often he sat with his head bowed.

The congregation of the little church took a curious kind of pride in Max's devotion to Irene. Few people had known them when she was totally herself, and Max wasn't much of a conversationalist, though he seemed eager to exchange pleasantries if approached. But his gentleness and patience with Irene showed that theirs was a special relationship. Most husbands wouldn't have tried to care for a wife in that condition by themselves for so many years — at home, let alone in public — but he always brought Irene to church dinners, potlucks, and programs, as well as to worship. No one acknowledged the toll his constant attention to Irene was taking on Max. They only saw how well he coped, and praised him for his loving faithfulness.

But when the pastor called on him at home, Max shared his loneliness and confusion.

"I struggle with my conscience every day, Pastor, because I want it to be over. For years I prayed to God for a miracle, or a medical cure that would bring Irene back to me, the way she used to be. Now I just pray for an end to it. I used to talk to her all day long, just like I always had, in case she could hear me. It scared me to think she might know everything that's going on, but not be able to tell me. Then, one day, I looked into her eyes while I was making some silly comment, and I just stopped, right in the middle of the sentence. Her eyes were totally empty. There was no life inside. When we got married we vowed it would be until death do us part, but I don't know how much longer I can keep this up. The days are so long, and I have to be there for her every minute. The doctors say she could go on this way for years. It's like she's dead, but I can't mourn her and go on with my life because she's still here. Does that make any sense? Some days I don't even want to get out of bed.

I'm so lonely,'' he said. ''I wish I had something to live for again.''

There was a long, uncomfortable silence. The pastor didn't really know what to say. Finally he took Max's hand and suggested that they pray together for guidance.

Within six months, Max filed for a divorce and put Irene into the local nursing home. There were exclamations of shock and dismay at his actions from the church and community, until people began to notice the change in Max. He was smiling and laughing again. His hair and clothes were neater, he had a new lightness in his step, and he looked years younger. He began seeing a widow lady from out in the county who frequently came to the Senior Citizens' center. Evelyn, who had been mourning her late husband for several years, looked happier, too. Max brought her to church for worship and dinners and programs. They joined a square dance group for Seniors, and twice a week they spent the afternoon at the nursing home, sitting with Irene and helping to care for her. When the divorce was final, they went to the pastor to ask him to marry them.

''After our last talk, I thought long and hard about my life with Irene, and I prayed a lot,'' Max said. ''We were together for 48 years: during the last six she didn't even know me. With every year that passed, I lost a little more hope . . . a little more of myself. I decided that I couldn't go on taking care of her, because it was killing me. You know that I believe in the vows about being married until death do us part. I still love Irene, but she's not there anymore. She's dead. I figure maybe God will understand what I've done.'' He turned and smiled at his companion. ''So, after I thought it out, I filed for a divorce and signed Irene into the nursing home. I've felt like a new man ever since. And then I met Evelyn.''

''We would like to share what's left of our lives with one another,'' Evelyn said shyly. ''Do you think that would be a bad thing?''

———————————

Story Questions

1. Do you think divorce and remarriage in this story is a "bad thing"? What could Max have done differently? How could the townspeople and the church have been more supportive?

2. The story of Max and Irene is based on a true story. Consider the following letter about a similar true story which appeared in one of Ann Landers' columns in 1991. Does the truth of one story belie the truth of the other? Is what Max does less loving than what the man described in the letter does?

Dear Ann Landers: I'm going to tell you about a love story that I witness every time I go to the nursing home to see my husband who has Alzheimer's disease. Unfortunately, I know firsthand how this terrible illness affects family members, but I would like the world to know what love really is.

I see a man who, I understand, has spent the last eight years caring for his wife who has Alzheimer's. They have been married over 50 years. He cooks and feeds her every bite of food she eats. He has bathed her and dressed her every day all these years. They have no other family. She lost a baby at birth and they never had any more children.

I cannot describe the tenderness and love that man shows for his wife. She is unable to recognize anyone, including him. The only things she shows any interest in are two baby dolls. They are never out of her hands.

I observed him when I parked my car beside his the other day. He sat in his old pickup truck for a few minutes, then he patted down what little hair he had, straightened the threadbare collar of his shirt and looked in the mirror for a final check before going in to see his wife. It was as if he were courting her. They have been partners all these years and have seen each other under all kinds of circumstances, yet he carefully groomed himself before he called on his wife, who wouldn't even know him.

This is an example of true love and commitment the world needs today.

— Fort Worth

3. As many as 4 million Americans are believed to be suffering from Alzheimer's disease, and at the present time there is no cure (Gelman/Hager/Quade 54). Its victims have been described as being lost in their own minds. Have you known anyone who has suffered from this disease? Tell about your experience.

4. With the Baby Boom generation moving into middle age, it is projected that the number of Alzheimer cases could rise to 14 million by the year 2050 (54). If you learned that you had Alzheimer's disease, or other physically or mentally disabling diseases like Parkinson's Disease, or Multiple Sclerosis, what would your wishes be concerning your care? What instructions would you give your spouse/loved ones? Would divorce be one of the options you would suggest?

Digging Into The Text

He left that place and went to the region of Judea and beyond the Jordan. And crowds again gathered around him: and, as was his custom, he again taught them. Some Pharisees came, and to test him they asked, "Is it lawful for a man to divorce his wife?" He answered them, "What did Moses command you?" They said, "Moses allowed a man to write a certificate of dismissal and to divorce her." But Jesus said to them, "Because of your hardness of heart he wrote this commandment for you. But from the beginning of creation, 'God made them male and female.' For this reason a man shall leave his father and mother and be joined to his wife, and the two shall become one flesh. Therefore, what God has joined together, let no one separate." Then in the house the disciples asked him again about this matter. He said to them, "Whoever divorces his wife and marries another commits adultery against her; and if she divorces her husband and marries another, she commits adultery."

Mark 10:1-12

The confrontation in Mark 10:1-12, between the Pharisees and Jesus, begins as a question on Jewish law and ends as a lesson in the faults of human nature. The Pharisees are offended and threatened by the way Jesus' teachings diverge from traditional interpretation of Jewish law, and they want to trap him. If Jesus has already commented on divorce in his teachings, and contradicts himself in answering the Pharisees' question, he will discredit himself. If he condemns divorce while preaching within the territory governed by Herod Antipas — who had indeed divorced his wife to marry his brother's wife, and whom John the Baptist was beheaded for chastising — Jesus could likewise be put to death. And if he contradicts the law of Moses, the Pharisees can charge him with heresy. But Jesus goes beyond the question asked of him about divorce to God's original intent for marriage — that of lifetime companionship — the spiritual fusing of two beings into one flesh. This is the crux of the problem in divorce. His final words on the subject are even those used in the traditional wedding vows of today: "Therefore, what God has joined together, let no one separate" (Mark 10:9).

Jesus labels the human imperfection which made Moses' law about divorce necessary as "hardening of the heart." William Barclay, in his commentary on the Gospel of Mark, suggests that Moses' law may have been given not as a permission for divorce, but to attempt to control the divorces that were already rampant among the Hebrews. His law could have been meant to make divorce more difficult by imposing upon it specific rules and procedures (240). The rabbinical interpretations of the law in Jesus' time covered both extremes. The conservatives permitted divorce only in the case of adultery. The liberals would permit it for female offenses as incidental as burning the bread or being less desirable than another woman. Of course, men were the only ones permitted to seek divorce in Jewish society, because women were considered property, not beings with rights.

A major emphasis of Jesus' ministry was the recognition of women as persons. Halford E. Luccock, in his exposition on Mark 10:1-12, calls Jesus a champion of women, whom he looked upon as people, not chattels. He says Jesus clearly goes against the customs and prevailing ideas of male dominance in Hebrew thought and practice to give the world "a new conception of women as persons equal with men in the sight of God" (795). The Jewish practice of divorce in Jesus' time and before was a cruel and unfair misuse of women. Jesus wanted to see women treated with more respect and equality. But this was only one portion of his objection to divorce. The spirit in which his people were entering into marriage was the major concern.

In answering the Pharisees "loaded" question, Jesus addresses not divorce itself, but God's original intention for the institution of marriage. What he accomplishes is, in effect, going over the heads of both the Pharisees and Moses to the one true authority ... God. Jesus points out that God intended marriage to be forever . . . a fusing of flesh which makes two people one person. And because the two are one, no one — not man, woman, Moses, or the Pharisees — should separate them. The King James Version of the Bible uses the words "put asunder" in that portion of verse 9. One of the dictionary meanings for "asunder" is "in pieces," which is literally what both parties of a divorce should be in if they entered the marriage covenant in the spirit intended by God. Clearly, in most cases of divorce that is true of at least one of the partners. And Jesus takes a very hard line when the disciples question him further on the issue. He states emphatically that if a man divorces his wife and marries another woman, he is committing adultery. Mark adds, for the benefit of his Roman and Greek readers, for whom divorce was an option for women as well as men, that a woman who divorces her husband and marries again is also committing adultery. If he is to make his point clearly, there is no other stance Jesus can take. God did not make allowance for divorce; humans did, out of their own hardness of heart which would not permit them to remain one with the person they married, or because they entered into marriage in the wrong spirit or for the wrong reasons.

In light of his stance, then, did Jesus condemn all who divorced and remarried? Does God condemn them? What about the innocent party who does not want divorce, but has it thrust upon him or her by the spouse? Those who interpret Jesus' statement on divorce as the absolute law on the subject would condemn them all. But Luccock states that Jesus was not trying to establish a new legalism or make himself a newer, greater Pharisee, and that those who think he was should consider his words in John 14:9: "Have you been with me so long, and yet you do not know me?" (797). Joseph Fletcher, in *Situation Ethics,* says: ". . . when the motive of the law observer is to hide behind the letter of the law in order to escape the higher demands of its spirit or to escape the complexities of responsible decision, that is cheap legalism" (83). And Paul Tillich, in *Morality and Beyond,* looks at law in light of love:

... love liberates us from the bondage to absolute ethical traditions to conventional morals, and to authorities that claim to know the right decisions, perhaps without having listened to the demand of the unique moment. The Spirit is the Spirit of newness. It breaks the prison of any absolute moral law, even when vested with the authority of a sacred tradition. Love can reject as well as utilize every moral tradition, and it always scrutinizes the validity of moral convention (43).

The theme of the entirety of Jesus' life and ministry can be summed up in that one word· love. Jesus identifies human faults and failures in divorce, considering what God intended for marriage to be from the beginning, but he continually emphasizes God's love and forgiveness. Dwight Hervey Small, in *The Right To Remarry*, clarifies Jesus' stance in light of God's intention:

God's original intent, expressed in the orders of Creation in Genesis, envisions marriage as indissoluable. It is an exclusive contract of life-partnership, embracing the union of two persons and a surcease to loneliness ... the couple is "one flesh," an expression meant to speak of a total union of two persons in mind, body, and spirit. But when marriage fails to become a catalyst for human personality, the road to full self-realization, then marriage as intended does not exist ... The fidelity, the love, the self-sacrifice, and the devotion of husband and wife to each other and their children are meant to speak more clearly than words of Christ's love for the Church. But when this is nonexistent, then marriage as intended does not exist and it becomes difficult, if not impossible, to talk about what God has joined together (15 & 16).

How, then, are imperfect humans viewed by God in the event of a divorce? If we are to believe Jesus' teachings, we are viewed with the love and compassion of a father who knows and understands our weaknesses. The apostle Paul states emphatically, "For I am convinced that neither death, nor life, nor angels, nor rulers, nor things present, nor things to come, nor powers, nor height, nor depth, nor anything else in all creation, will be able to separate us from the love of God in Christ Jesus our Lord'' (Romans 8:38-39). God's understanding of human frailty and imperfection, and God's never-ending love displayed through Jesus, are our comfort. No one is cut off from God's love. This is an important fact to remember in a world where absolutes are so much in demand. So, what is our obligation to those who suffer the agony of having their marriages and lives reduced to ''pieces''? In Jesus' own example, it is unquestionably to comfort them with Christian love.

Digging Into The Text Questions

1. How was divorce viewed in your family when you were growing up? If you feel comfortable sharing, tell about a divorce that had an impact on your early life.

2. What are some reasons people have for divorce today that would not have been considered by your parents or grandparents?

3. Can you think of an instance in which a divorce would be the most loving solution to a couple's marital problems? Discuss how each of the following reasons for divorce is or is not a good reason:

a. Woman's career
b. Seeking a perfect mate
c. AIDS
d. Infertility
e. Career conflict
f. Infidelity

4. How might divorce be the most loving choice considering the following incidents?

a. Incest
b. Physical/sexual abuse
c. Hopeless coma
d. Lingering/totally disabling disease
e. Criminal activity
f. Alcoholism
g. Repeated, unrepentant infidenlity
h. Drug abuse

5. If, as Jesus says, "Whoever divorces ... and marries another commits adultery," should the church forbid divorce in all circumstances, or should divorced persons be accepted and forgiven, as are all sinners who are part of the body of Christ?

Works Cited

Barclay, William. *The Daily Bible Series: The Gospel of Mark*. Philadelphia: Westminster, 1975.

Buber, Martin. *Tales of the Hasidim: Later Masters.* Trans. Olga Marx. New York: Schocken Books, 1948.

Fletcher, Joseph. *Situation Ethics: The New Morality*. Philadelphia: Westminster, 1966.

Gelman, David, with Mary Hager and Vicki Quade. "The Brain Killer." *Newsweek*. 18 Dec. 1989: 54-56.

Luccock, Halford E. "Exposition on the Gospel According to St. Mark." *The Interpreter's Bible.* 12 vols. New York: Abingdon, 1951.

Small, Dwight Hervey, *The Right to Remarry*. Old Tappan: Fleming H. Revell Co., 1975.

Tillich, Paul. *Morality and Beyond*. New York: Harper & Row, 1963.

Chapter 5

Suffer The Little Children

Jesus said, "Suffer little children, and forbid them not, to come unto me: for of such is the kingdom of heaven." And he laid his hands on them, and departed thence. Matthew 19:13-15 KJV

He had seen them through the big front window of the bar, edging their game of catch closer and closer to the alley, taking their time, shouting and causing plenty of ruckus to appear normal; but he knew what they were up to. When the beer truck sounded its horn to clear the alleyway the shouting and jeering faded. Mac laid down the bar towel and eased his bulk into the back room. He waited beside the delivery door, watching as quietly as his overweight wheezing would permit, until the door handle turned ever so slightly and stopped, then turned again and began to ease open. First a tousled red head eased through the crack in the door, then a nappy black one, peering into the darkness, willing their eyes to adjust so they could see the treasure they sought — six- and 12-packs of beer and pints and quarts of any kind of liquor — anything they could carry off quickly that would bring them a few dollars.

Mac shook his head as he watched them edge in a little more. Damned brats were getting bolder and bolder. Used to be teenagers, punks and gang members, who would try to break in for some free booze. Now it was 8- and 9-year-old profiteers! The times were changing. There was much impatient whispering and shoving from behind the two scouts, and Mac took advantage of their distraction. When they turned to beat back the eager looters, he wrenched open the door and began hollering at the top of his gravelly bass voice. There were numerous cries of terror as the gang of youngsters froze, then reconnected

69

with their muscles and scattered in every direction. Mac chased them down the alley, grabbing futilely at the fleeing forms, but his great midsection got in the way as one after another ducked under it and even through his legs to escape. Only one, a tiny, straggly-haired blonde girl, slipped on the damp alley pavement and fell. She cried out as the cement peeled away several layers of skin on her knees, then cowered in terror as Mac's shadow blocked out the light above her.

"Come on, get up!" the bartender growled, stooping with a grunt to set the small thief on her feet. But as his hands reached out to pick her up, her frail arms flew up reflexively to cover her head. She seemed as surprised to have been helped up, not hit, as he was that she had expected him to hit her. Mac looked at her, trembling before him, her back to the wall, blood running down her scrawny legs from the fresh scrapes on her knees, and saw for the first time the bruises on her upper arms where mean fingers had dug in, and the purple splotch along her left jawline. Her flimsy, sleeveless summer dress was too short, though it hung loosely on her bony frame. The blonde hair that lay matted against her neck hadn't been washed in weeks, and her bare feet were black-bottomed. He had been about to tell her to go home and get her knees taken care of, but he knew that they wouldn't be, so he held out his hand.

"Come on inside with me. I'll get you some Band-Aids for your knees."

The girl's huge blue eyes leaked tears down her face leaving trails of white through the dirt, and narrowed as she considered his offer. Although she wasn't yet six, she knew that if she went home she would have to wash the blood from her knees herself. There were no Band-Aids, and there was no more food in her apartment now than there had been at breakfast or at noon. Her stomach was rumbling uncomfortably. If she woke Mama before Mama woke up by herself, she'd get hit. If there was a man with Mama, she'd get hit twice as hard. Her knees hurt and she was weak from hunger. She put her hand into the big man's hand and hobbled after him through the back door of the bar.

Mac snorted in disgust as he lifted the filthy child onto the end of the bar and went to get the first aid kit and a clean, wet towel. He'd never cared much for kids — not his own, who were grown now, and especially not other people's who stole from him and caused him trouble. But like her or not, this poor little ragamuffin tugged at Mac's heart. She was so little. Somebody should be telling her bedtime stories. Somebody should put ribbons in her hair and buy her dolls and shiny black shoes. Nobody did anything for this child. She was dirty and she smelled bad and her stomach was growling so loudly he could hear it from the cash register, where he pulled a bag of pretzels off the display rack and carried it back to her with the first aid kit.

A few mid-afternoon customers began to filter in out of the heat and Mac washed his hands and waited on them. The girl stayed where he had put her, on the back end of the bar, munching down pretzels so fast she was almost inhaling them. When her knees were cleaned, disinfected and bandaged, he sat her on a barstool and gave her more pretzels and a glass of orange juice. Between customers he drifted back to check on her. The third time he went, she was sound asleep, her head resting on her arms on the bar. Mac wasn't sure what to do with her. He didn't know where she lived, if one could call it that, and he couldn't leave her where she was for fear she'd fall and hurt herself. So he lifted her, pretzel bag and all, and carried her featherweight body into the back room. He threw his old winter parka down in a corner and laid her on it, and she nestled herself inside without ever opening her eyes. He didn't want to just leave her there, but he had customers and it would only get busier as evening came. As usual, he thought ironically, she was on her own.

When the nighttime bartender came in at 6:00, Mac took a break and went back to check on the girl. The little nest she had made in the parka was still warm, but she was gone. Although she had unlocked the alley door to get out, she had closed and latched it carefully from the outside. Mac scratched his thinning hair and shook his head. Poor little thing had gone home. He hoped she was all right.

Business was usually brisk at Mac's Bar. He lived alone in the little apartment above, so he spent much of his day cleaning, doing bookwork, inventorying his stock. Mac had owned the bar for 23 years, so he knew the neighborhood. He also knew how it was changing — becoming run-down. There were so many people with so little hope in their lives, and he heard their stories when they came in to spend a little change on a draft beer and bend his ear. Of course that was one of the reasons Mac owned a bar; he was a listener, a commiserator with the miserable. He knew his regular customers, and his regular customers knew about the neighborhood. So he began asking that night about the girl.

It was the usual story, when he finally found someone who knew it. Her mother wasn't married and lived on welfare and what she could get from men she picked up in bars at night. She used drugs and might be addicted. She said she loved her daughter, but she had no idea how to care for the child. And the child, less than six years old, often cared for the mother, who was probably less than 20. Mac shook his head sadly, and from that night on he watched for the girl.

It was two days before Mac spotted the child again. She was sitting on the steps of an apartment building across the street and half a block up from the bar, watching older children play stickball. When they drifted down the street, she followed, although they were not including her in their group. No doubt that was how she had come to be in the alley when the gang of hooligans had tried to loot his back room. She followed them around so she had a place to be. As the crowd of children rushed past the open door of the bar, Mac pushed his bulk out into the sun. His shadow once again covered the scrawny child as she trailed after the others, and she looked up in surprise at Mac's hulking frame. There was blood caked around one of her tiny nostrils, and a fresh bruise under her left eye. Her wariness relaxed when she looked at Mac's concerned face.

"Did you have anything to eat this morning?" he growled, and she shook her head. He held out his hand and she put hers into it without hesitation and followed him into the coolness of the bar.

"What's your name?" Mac asked after he had lifted her onto a barstool and brought her orange juice.

"Gracie," she said in the very soft voice of one practiced at being inconspicuous.

"Hmmmph. I thought all little girls nowadays were named Crystal and Tiffany and Amber and Danielle. I like Gracie. That's a good name."

The little face blossomed into a radiant smile, which displayed the absence of her two front teeth with their jagged-edged replacements just emerging into view. "That was my grandma's name — Grace."

"Do you get to go visit your grandma?"

"She's gone to heaven. We used to live with her, and she made me cookies and let me play with her jewelry."

"Did your grandma give you a bath and comb your hair?"

The child's blue eyes flooded over with tears and she looked down in shame at her dirty dress with her long, skinny, dirty legs protruding from beneath. Mac felt like an ogre for making her cry.

"Come on," he said gruffly. "Let's go to the store." He removed his apron, hung the "out to lunch" sign on the door, though it was only 9:00 a.m., and took the little girl's hand in his as they headed up the street to the dime store.

Gracie picked out a kiddie bubble bath, some crayons and a coloring book, and a folder of paper dolls when Mac told her she could buy whatever she wanted to take back and play with at the bar. Then he picked out shampoo, a new dress, some sandals, underwear, and a pair of shorts and T-shirt with the saleswoman's help. Back at the bar, he got down the old galvanized tub he sometimes used to ice cans and bottles of beer for large parties in the bar and turned it into a makeshift bathtub. He couldn't take the girl upstairs during business hours to wash her in his own bathtub, so he made do. Mac had never seen a child so content with so little. While she soaked and played in the warm water and bubbles, he washed out her filthy clothes, fixed her a sandwich and some fruit and cookies, and tackled washing and brushing the snarls from her wispy hair. She never complained, though at times it appeared he was going to pull the hair right out by the roots trying to remove the matted tangles. When he dried her off with one of his own threadbare bath towels, he was shocked anew at the way her ribs protruded and at the number of bruised spots on her translucent skin. But afterward, in her new clothes with her hair dry and shiny, and curling in surprising little tendrils around her face and neck, she looked radiant and very happy.

Mac gave her permission to move the empty crates and old pieces of furniture around in the empty corner of the store room, then went to work as the regulars began to shuffle in at 11:00. When he looked in on her occasionally, she was coloring or talking to the paper dolls she punched out, using painstaking care not to rip the beautiful paper clothing. At 1:30, when he brought her milk and cookies, she was sound asleep on his old winter parka in the corner.

At first he used to watch for her to come out of her apartment building in the mornings and stand in the doorway to wave her over for breakfast. Then, gradually, she grew bold enough to cross the street and enter the open door on her own. When she had eaten, it was understood that she was welcome to play in the back room for as long as she wanted. Sometimes she would disappear for an hour or two, but she always came back and stayed until 6:00 p.m. Mac never said much, and Gracie didn't ask too many questions. But the relationship between them grew to be so comfortable that one day, when she went into the back to play after breakfast and found a baby doll with changeable clothes, she came right back into the bar, climbed onto Mac's lap as he sat at one of the tables reading his morning paper, and put her arms around his neck to give him a long, uninhibited hug, which he returned with equal abandon.

"I love you, Mac," she whispered into his chest.

"I love you, too, Gracie," he returned in his gravelly growl.

Gracie arranged a thoughtfully planned playhouse in Mac's back room. Empty crates became shelves, tables and a bed. Mac provided pillows, blankets, and new toys occasionally. He even brought down an old color television from his apartment and hooked up an antenna so she could watch *Sesame Street*. Gracie never entered the bar when there were customers, using the alley door to exit and enter instead. Mac added to her wardrobe as the need arose, and pieces of clothing and toys began to appear from her apartment. He watched as closely as he could, but never saw her mother, or anyone he thought to be her mother, enter or leave the apartment building during the day. At night he was too busy to keep track.

The regular customers began to remark about all of the brightly colored pictures and artwork Mac was suddenly displaying around the edges of the backbar. Mac only grunted when they asked if it was from his grandchildren, or expressed surprise that he even had grandchildren. He had never talked about them with the customers because he had never met them. But he didn't bother to say so. Nowadays thoughts of his own family brought back disturbing memories of Margaret's early death, the ache inside himself, mirrored in his children's eyes, too much drinking, bickering, shouting, hitting and crying. Whenever he saw a new bruise on Gracie, images of his own children cringing beneath his upraised hand haunted him. He had never considered himself a bad father, but when his children had left home, they had left him behind them, for good. Mac loved Gracie, and delighted in her affection for him in his own reserved way. Gracie displayed her affection as openly and innocently as any five-year-old, initiating whatever hugs, kisses, or lapsittings she needed, when she needed them, to make up for his reserve. But the more attached Mac grew to her, the more uneasy he became, because he knew their happiness couldn't last.

It was in August, during the hottest days of summer, that he first noticed them going door to door — a woman and a man, accompanied by two policemen. Gracie had had her breakfast and was playing in the back room, as usual. He had heard her singing "Jesus Loves Me" to her baby doll when he checked on her last, and had determined to ask her if she used to go to Sunday school. He himself wasn't a church-going man. His occupation and his cynicism toward life had always prevented him from joining up with a group of people who were bent on eliminating livelihoods like his. Yet he had always talked with the Lord when he had troubles. Since Gracie had come into his life, he had carried on practically non-stop conversations on one topic or another. And though he never would have admitted it to anyone, the words that most frequently flowed from his mind to God's were, "Please, don't let anything happen to my Gracie. Keep her safe, and don't let anyone take her away from me."

Mac could sense that that was what the woman and man with the police officers would do long before they got to his place. It was a twisting, aching, sinking feeling deep inside his massive gut that wouldn't go away. Something had happened to change Gracie's life, and it would change his as well. He could hear the faint strains of the "Barney" theme song playing as the woman and man entered the front door of the bar. "I love you, you love me, we're a happy family ..."

"Excuse me, are you the owner of this bar?" the woman asked, and when he grunted yes in reply, continued, "We're from the child welfare bureau, and we're looking for Grace Ellen Powell. She's about six years old and has blonde hair and blue eyes. She lives with her mother in an apartment across the street, but we haven't been able to locate her. Have you seen the child?"

"What's the problem?" Mac asked, evading the question.

"Her mother was arrested last night for prostitution and possession of a controlled substance. She'll be held in jail until her preliminary hearing, and she told us her child would be alone. We're trying to locate her to place her in protective custody."

Mac saw the woman's eyes surveying the displays of artwork around the backbar and heaved a heavy sigh. Then he motioned for the couple to follow and led them to the back room door. He held a finger to his lips before he pushed it open, and both nodded in assent. What they saw through the door was a miniature living room in which a beautiful little blonde girl sat watching a children's show on television with her baby doll. She alternately sang along, sucked her thumb and rocked in silent attention, and spoke to her doll about what she had heard. The adults backed away quietly and Mac led them back into the bar and seated them at one of the tables with glasses of ice water.

"Gracie's been coming here for over two months. I feed her and clean her clothes and buy her little things when she needs them. She comes and goes to her apartment as she pleases. She never comes into the bar when there are customers, and she always goes home at night. I've never seen her mother, but I know she hits her, 'cause she's always bruised. I know a bar ain't a good place to raise a child 'cause I raised three of my own right upstairs, but I keep her safe here, and Gracie and I have gotten used to one another. Is there any way she can stay with me? It might scare her to have to go to a strange place, with people she don't know. And to tell the truth, it would break my heart to lose her. I've got plenty of room upstairs that she's never even seen, and I'll follow whatever guidelines you set up. Is there a chance we can stay together? Is there a chance I can keep her at least until you know what's going to happen to her mother?"

The social workers hadn't expected anything like this. A tiny, high-pitched voice began to sing along with the Barney theme song as the show ended, "I love you, you love me, we're best friends as friends should be ...."

"Could we talk with the child?" the woman asked.

"Gracie, come in here!" Mac growled. They all heard the door to the back room open, and the child skipped into the bar, then saw them and stopped as if to retreat. "It's okay," Mac said, motioning her forward. "These folks need to talk to you."

Gracie narrowed her blue eyes to size up the strangers, then approached the table confidently, climbed into Mac's lap and nestled against him comfortably. As her partner began to ask the child questions, the woman watched Gracie and the bartender together. Their close relationship was a complete surprise. They had seen the squalor of the apartment where the child lived, yet she was clean and appeared well fed. The little play room was simple and neat and appropriate for a child in spite of the fact that it was surrounded by cases of liquor. And this gruff old man, whose voice and curtness made she herself hesitate, had bared his soul to them in hopes of keeping this child he obviously loved. No, this wouldn't be easy. Nothing here was what she had expected. If he were a blood relative it wouldn't be a problem, but the Bureau had its rules and regulations.

Mac looked from one caseworker to the other as Gracie answered the questions about her home, her mother, how she was treated, and how she felt about Mac. "Please, God," he prayed inside his head, "please don't let them take my Gracie away."

But, in the end, they had. The welfare woman had apologized, saying she wished she could leave them together, but explaining that there were rules and regulations. Gracie had looked stubborn at first, narrowing her eyes and screwing up her lips in a tough sneer, but when she saw defeat on Mac's face, and the wet redness of his eyes, she broke into sobs and clung to him.

The social worker watched in admiration as Mac comforted her, helped her pack a bag of her belongings, and reassured her that he would visit her: that they would always be friends. Then the two caseworkers took Gracie and left.

It was several weeks before Mac learned of Gracie's foster home placement, 15 miles away in another borough of the city. He took a bus, transferred three times and had to walk five blocks, but he kept his promise to visit her. Gracie was glad to see him, but she seemed happy in her new home. There was a cat and a dog, and her foster parents had two older foster children and a baby. They weren't rich, but their home was clean and comfortable, and it wasn't a bar. Mac tried to feel happy for the child, but his own heartbreak interfered.

Standing alone at the big front window of the bar one September morning, when the north wind was blowing in a promise of a harsh winter to come, Mac continued to bemoan his loneliness and disappointment to God in his mind. "Why did you have to send her to me for such a short time? Why did you let me get attached to her if I had to let her go? Why couldn't things have stayed the way they were? It's better not to get attached to people and things. It's better to keep to yourself."

And yet, that very morning Mac had looked up the number of his youngest daughter in the telephone directory and had called her. She was surprised to hear from him — suspicious about what he wanted, but she hadn't hung up on him. He had told her he just wanted to know how she was. She had said fine, and thanked him for the call. Since he was a man of few words, that had been all he could muster for a first conversation, but he knew he'd call again. Maybe one day he'd even try the other two, if Margie had their phone numbers.

Mac mused about relationships as he dried freshly washed bar glasses and studied Gracie's artwork, still tacked around the backbar. A new picture had arrived in yesterday's mail, along with a photograph — Gracie's kindergarten school picture. It hadn't occurred to Mac that the reason the streets were so quiet was that school had begun. Maybe his liquor stock would be safe now, at least until Christmas vacation.

That was when he had wandered to the front window again, and looked out, across the street at the steps of the apartment where Gracie used to live. A woman swept open the building's front door and half dragged, half lifted a small boy after her by one arm. She appeared to be shouting at him, though Mac couldn't hear her with the door closed. She shook him once, waved her arms at the streets in both directions, and shoved him toward the steps, giving him a hard swat on the behind for good measure. Then she looked around, smoothed back her hair, and straightened the short, tight-fitting dress she wore as a fancy car pulled up and a dark, well-dressed man got out and opened the passenger door for her. She reached back inside the apartment door for a short, furry coat and purse, stepped regally down the stairs past the boy to the waiting car, and left without a backward glance.

The boy sat down on the steps and buried his head in his knees, his shoulders shaking with sobs, but after a minute he raised his head again, swiped his arm under his nose, and rose to walk down the steps. He crossed the street, heading up toward the bar slowly, with his hands in the pockets of the windbreaker that wasn't warm enough to fend off the north wind. As he drew closer, Mac saw that his nose was still running. He was even smaller than Gracie, maybe four, or just barely five. His nappy brown hair and creamy, coffee-colored skin made it clear that his other parent was black.

"So many of them," Mac grumbled, tossing down the bar towel and lumbering toward the front door. "No one to love them; no one to care for them; no one to feed them. Why?" His anger at the Child Welfare Bureau flared. They took Gracie away from him when she was being well cared for, but they left this poor moppet on the street. Where would he go? What would he do all day? Who would watch out for him until his mother came back, if she bothered? He didn't know where the line came from — somewhere in the Bible, he was sure — but it kept repeating itself over and over in his mind. "Suffer the little children to come unto me."

As he opened the front door of the bar and inserted his bulk in the path of the very small boy, it suddenly occurred to Mac that that was the key: children, not just one child. The tub and the television and the crates were still sitting unused in his back room. His heart was empty, as well.

"Looks like you need a handkerchief, kid," Mac growled, extending his hand with one in it toward the startled little face that gazed up past his massive midsection at his large face, which wore a tender look that belied the gruffness of his voice. "You cold?"

The brown eyes studied him uncertainly, then the little head nodded.

"Your ma give you anything to eat before she left?"

The eyes drifted back to the empty front of his apartment building where the car had been, then sank down to the sidewalk by his feet as he shook his head.

"Come on," Mac said, with no further formality, extending his hand to the child and holding open the bar door. "I'll make you a sandwich and some hot chocolate."

The brown eyes scrutinized him again, then a draft of heat from inside the building struck the cold, hungry child and his mind was made up for him. He inserted his icy little hand into Mac's ham-sized grip and stepped into the warm bar.

———————————

Story Questions

1. Why would an abused child like Gracie voluntarily return to her abusive parent when she had found a safe haven?

2. What risk was Mac running in harboring this abused child?

3. Why do you suppose the child welfare bureau removed Gracie from Mac's protective care?

4. Do you believe that the practice of keeping children with their biological parents is always the best plan?

5. Have you ever suspected a family member, friend or acquaintance of physically, emotionally, or sexually abusing his/her child? What did you do?

6. What is our responsibility as individuals if we learn of accused or suspected abuse situations? What is our responsibility as the church?

7. What are some advantages and disadvantages of Mac's approach to intervention? What more could he have done? What would you do?

Digging Into The Text

If any of you put a stumbling block before one of these little ones who believe in me, it would be better for you if a great millstone were fastened around your neck and you were drowned in the depth of the sea.

Matthew 18:6 NRSV

Then there were brought unto him little children that he should put his hands on them and pray: and the disciples rebuked them. But Jesus said, "Suffer little children, and forbid them not, to come unto me: for of such is the kingdom of heaven." And he laid his hands on them, and departed thence.   Matthew 19:13-15 KJV

In this story beginning at Matthew 18:1, Jesus sets a child among the disciples and tells them that in order to see the kingdom of heaven, they must "change and become like children." Imagine the disciples' surprise. They, who have been given the power to heal the sick and lame, give sight to the blind and hearing to the deaf, cast out demons and even raise the dead, are suddenly expected to see that a mere child is fit for the kingdom and they are not. Their surprise stems not only from their power as disciples, but from the fact that their perception of the kingdom of heaven is in error. They have been vying for first place in Jesus' esteem so that they can sit at his right and left hands in his kingdom. Jesus tells them that they don't understand what they are asking for, referring to the suffering and death on the cross that he knows will usher in his kingdom. Therefore, he gives them the example of the child as a model of greatness for his kingdom. Matthew's account goes further, having Jesus declare that if any of *them* put a stumbling block before a child who believes in him, they would be better off weighted with a millstone and drowned in the depths of the sea. Woe to the one by whom the stumbling block comes! (Matthew 18:1-7).

This is a heavy warning from the light of the world. After all, in that day, although children were a man's posterity, they were also his property, along with his wife, cattle and other possessions. Children were unfinished vessels to be molded and shaped, and they were subject to the father's will and decisions. Jesus makes them so much more. In his eyes, it is the innocence, wonder, trust and humility that children possess, and his disciples lack, that fit them for heaven. William Barclay, in his commentary on the gospel of Matthew, states:

> *To the child a state of dependence is perfectly natural ... He is perfectly content to be utterly dependent on those who love him and care for him. If men [and women] would accept the fact of their dependence on God, a new strength and a new peace would enter their lives ... The child's humility is the pattern of the Christian's behavior to his fellow [human beings] and the child's dependence and trust are the pattern of the Christian attitude toward God ... (176).*

If, as Jesus warned, one who causes a child who believes in him to stumble deserves to have a millstone hung around his or her neck and be drowned in the depths of the sea, what about us? Have Americans of the dawning twenty-first century eliminated stumbling blocks for children?

According to estimates of the National Committee to Prevent Child Abuse, 1 million American children were neglected or abused in 1993. This means 15 of every 1,000 children suffered maltreatment (Associated Press 33). During the nine years the Committee has been compiling figures, the annual rate of child abuse fatalities has risen 50%, with most of the increase occurring between 1985-86, the year that crack cocaine became the drug of choice on American streets (Will 7). Approximately 2.9 million children were subjects of reports of possible neglect or abuse in 1993, with about 34% of cases substantiated. Of 47% of the reports which involved suspected child neglect, 30% were reports of physical abuse, 11% child sexual abuse, and 2% emotional maltreatment (Associated Press 33).

The Carnegie Corporation, a 30-member panel of experts in medicine, business, education and other fields, recently reported on a 3-year study of the greatest risk factors affecting many of the 12 million American children under age 3. Those risks include:

1. More than 25% of all births are to unmarried mothers;
2. Almost half of all children can expect to experience a divorce during childhood and to live an average of 5 years in a single-parent family;
3. Nearly 3 million children under age 3 live in families with incomes below the federal poverty level;
4. More than 5 million infants and toddlers are being cared for by other adults while their parents work. Care is often substandard;
5. Nine out of every 1,000 infants die before age one — a mortality rate higher than that of 19 other nations. Black babies are twice as likely as white babies to die in their first year;
6. As many as 60% of all 2-year-olds do not receive all necessary immunizations to prevent childhood diseases;
7. One in three victims of physical abuse is less than a year old (Dixon 15).

If the statistics aren't startling enough, the Committee adds these further grim findings:

1. As many as 6 million American infants and toddlers confront at least one of the above risk factors that could harm their future;
2. The first 3 years of life are crucial for laying the foundation for all that follows. During that time children should be with adults who offer nurturing love, protection, guidance, stimulation and support;
3. An adverse environment can compromise a young child's brain functions and overall development, placing the child at risk of developing a variety of cognitive, behavioral and physical difficulties, some of which may be irreversible;

4. More than half of mothers with children under 3 work outside the home, and most parents feel overwhelmed by dual demands of work and family, have less time to spend with children and worry about unreliable and substandard child care;

5. Families living in poverty also face lack of prenatal and child healthcare, human services and social support in increasingly violent neighborhoods, which further stacks the deck against their children;

6. Researchers believe early stress in children activates hormones that can impair learning and memory, causing intellectual and behavioral problems;

7. Seventy-three percent of teenaged mothers are unmarried, and 46% of all teenaged mothers go on welfare within 4 years of giving birth (Chira A1 +).

Why do citizens of one of the most socially and economically sound nations of the world rate so poorly when it comes to the care and nurture of our own children? The Carnegie Corporation cites poverty, divorce rates, births to unmarried mothers, and single-parent households as major contributing factors. The number of children entering foster care rose more than 50%, from 300,000 to 460,000, between 1987 and 1991. Reports of child abuse are rising, and an increasing number of small children grow up witnessing stabbings, shootings and beatings as everyday events (A11).

The support group Parents Anonymous provides clients with a list of factors that contribute to abusive behavior. Parents are more likely to abuse their children if:

1. They were abused as children and repeat their parents' behavior and patterns, continuing the cycle of abuse;

2. They have low self-esteem because of their own abuse and guilt over their behavior;

3. They feel isolated and lack support. Parents need someone to listen to them vent their feelings;

4. They feel overwhelmed by stress, crises, financial, marital or employment problems, or illness;

5. They perceive their child as "different" due to hyperactivity, learning disabilities or qualities they cannot accept which trigger stress or abuse;
6. They hold unrealistic expectations, in which they may project motives and capabilities onto their children of which they are not yet capable;
7. They use corporal punishment as a means of disciplining children, which, if it gets out of hand, may lead to physical abuse.

Generations of dysfunction, parents who are still children themselves, adults who cannot understand or empathize with a child's level of ability, people who learned from their own abuse and emulate their abusers, sufferers of sexual aberrations which draw them to children: all of these are stumbling blocks that are put before children even in our "enlightened" age. According to Jesus' evaluation of suitable punishment for such people, then, should those who physically, sexually or emotionally abuse children be drowned in the depths of the sea? Are they eternally damned? William Barclay's commentary brings out another helpful interpretation of the word "child" which puts Jesus' words in a different light:

> ... we must remember that the Jews used the word "child" in a double sense. They used it literally of the young child; but regularly a teacher's disciples were called his sons or his children. Therefore, a child also means a beginner in the faith, one who has just begun to believe, one who is not yet mature and established in the faith, one who has just begun on the right way and who may very easily be deflected from it. In this passage very often the child means both the young child and the beginner on the Christian way (177).

Jesus' warning, then, applied to each of his disciples in their interaction with the multitudes and with one another, just as it applies to *each one of us* in our interactions with one another. Barclay's interpretation would seem to warn us, as Jesus' words did the disciples, to take care who we influence and how we influence them. In the same token, we who consider ourselves staunch Christians should be aware that our faith may not be as steady as we think. Even the most righteous person can stumble if the stumbling block falls in an area we have previously been unaware of as weak. And woe to us if we are the cause of another's fall.

Therefore, we should all take warning as possible offenders, and we are all vulnerable as possible stumbling children. What should we see as our responsibility? First, we must protect the little children, because they are weak, vulnerable and unable to protect themselves. Second, we must report abusers, because their actions are harmful, because they need professional help, and because they are "children" of Christ for whom we have a moral responsibility. Abusers are often "adult children" who have been abused and who need understanding, guidance and compassion. Jesus would recognize their needs, and so should we. Third, we should examine our own attitudes and actions in light of the teachings of Christ. Like the disciples, we too often worry about who is the greatest and how to reach the top, and fail to recognize the humble path of service that leads to the kingdom of heaven.

Digging Into The Text Questions

1. What circumstances in today's society do you think have contributed most to the increases in child abuse and neglect?

2. What action or inaction by parents do you believe should warrant termination of parental rights? What dangers might that pose for "good" parents?

3. Do you believe in corporal punishment for children? Why or why not? Beginning at what age?

4. Have you ever been tempted to report, or have you ever reported, a parent you thought was abusive? What was the result?

5. What is our moral responsibility as Christians toward physically, emotionally or sexually abused children and youth?

6. What "stumbling blocks" does society as we know it put in the way of our Christian growth?

Works Cited

Associated Press. "Child Abuse Cases Reported at 1 Million." *The Kenosha News.* 8, Apr. 1994: 33.

Barclay, William. *The Gospel of Matthew: volume 2.* Philadelphia: Westminster Press, 1975: 175-177.

Chira, Susan. "Study Confirms Worst Fears on U.S. Children." *The New York Times.* 12, Apr. 1994: A1+.

Dixon, Jennifer. "Study Finds Many Troubled Toddlers." Associated Press. *The Kenosha News.* 13, Apr. 1994: 15.

Parents Anonymous. "Factors Contributing to Abusive Behavior."

Will, George. "Caulking Cracks in Abuse Prevention Costs A Lot." *The Kenosha News.* 3, May 1994: 7.

Chapter 6

If I Live To Be A Hundred

Do not cast me off in the time of old age; do not forsake me when my strength is spent.

Psalm 71:9

Sam Duncan lay in the semi-darkness of his nursing home room performing the only two activities of which he still considered himself capable: watching and waiting. Although his eyesight was dim, he could still make out the steady brightening of the light of dawn through the window next to his bed. And although his hearing was too far gone to catch the rumble of the medicine cart as it worked its way up the hall toward his room, he could sense that the time for his morning pills was near, and he waited for the nurse to push open the door and greet him and his roommate Arthur, who was still snoring loudly in the bed next to his.

Most of the accepted measures of quality of human existence no longer affected Sam. While time, in terms of years, seemed to slip away unnoticed, the hours of the day crept by in agonizing slowness. Time no longer meant anything to him. Schedules all belonged to the nurses and aides and family members who waited on him. He himself had no claim to time. The staff dieticians and cooks decided what he would eat, and when. The aides assigned to care for him on any given day decided when he would be bathed, dressed, shaved, and even toileted. His family decided what clothes he needed, what treats to bring to him, and when he should go out. The activity director decided when he needed exercise, stimulus and entertainment, and he was delivered into her hands by the aides upon request.

91

There were few days when Sam could tell you what had occurred the day before, or even the hour before. He had little memory for what he had eaten for dinner Tuesday or breakfast Saturday. He seldom knew the day of the week or the correct month, although seasons were still instinctively evident. The minutiae of every day had ceased to have meaning for him even before his nursing home days had begun ten years earlier, and he felt no concern or remorse over loss of interest in such trivia. But if you asked him if he remembered Pearl Harbor, or the day Franklin Roosevelt died, or what he was doing the day JFK was assassinated, he could tell you with detailed clarity what had gone on. He recalled vividly his wedding day, the day he and Martha buried their firstborn infant son, the details of the funeral of his grandson Sam who was killed in Vietnam, and what the weather was like on the day Martha died.

Sam also remembered the friends who had been most dear to him. They had all been gone for many years: Boots Martin, who had served with him in Germany in WWI; Alvy Hankins, who had gone to school with him and farmed outside of town; Dick Travis, who had been his business partner for nearly 40 years . . . all dead and buried long ago. It hadn't seemed unnatural that he had outlived them all, just part of life. But when he had outlived all of his children, the burden of life had become heavy, cumbersome. And now, at 102, it was nearly unbearable.

Sam had never been a complainer. Life was what it was. He didn't second-guess nature or the Creator. When he and Martha lost that first baby son, they had grieved and comforted one another, and eventually gone on with their lives. And God had blessed them with six healthy children who had survived well into old age. The death and destruction he had seen in the trenches during "the war to end all wars" was etched in his memory for all time, and yet he had survived it, both physically and emotionally. But when his grandson, young Samuel Wilks Duncan III, had been killed in Vietnam at the tender age of 19, it had taken much prayer and effort to overcome his sense of anger and grief. And when Martha died in 1984, at the ripe old age of 90, and his own heart beat on strong and steady, even though he knew it was broken, he had shaken a mental fist at God and demanded to know why. Why must he be left to bear the burdens of life alone? At 93, why couldn't he go home, too?

That had been ten years ago. Ten years of slowly declining health, gradual loss of sight, hearing, movement and body function. Ten years of being taken here and there, regardless of his own wishes, by those whose job it was to provide him with comfort, stimulation, and quality of life. His grandchildren became so busy with their own lives that they seldom visited. And when his last surviving daughter had died of cancer last year at the age of 75, Sam couldn't help but wonder if God was allowing him to be put to the test, as he did Job. He felt very keenly the truth of Jesus' words in the Gospel of John:

> ... when you were younger, you used to fasten your own belt and go wherever you wished. But when you grow old, you will stretch out your hands, and someone else will fasten a belt around you and take you where you do not wish to go.

And so Sam had formed a mental list of Psalms from which to pray in all of his various moods:

> How long, O Lord? Will you forget me forever? How long will you hide your face from me? How long must I bear pain in my soul, and have sorrow in my heart all day long?   Psalm 13:1-2

> My God, my God, why have you forsaken me? Why are you so far from helping me, from the words of my groaning? Oh my God, I cry by day, but you do not answer; and by night, but find no rest.   Psalm 22:1-2

93

Even though I walk through the valley of the shadow of death, I fear no evil; for you are with me; your rod and your staff — they comfort me. Psalm 23:4

As a deer longs for flowing streams, so my soul longs for you, O God. Psalm 42:1

Do not cast me off in the time of old age; do not forsake me when my strength is spent. For my enemies speak concerning me, and those who watch for my life consult together. Psalm 71:9-10

Sing praises to the Lord, O you his faithful ones, and give thanks to his holy name. For his anger is but for a moment; his favor is for a lifetime. Weeping may linger for the night, but joy comes with the morning.
Psalm 30:4-5

Joy comes with the morning . . . . Sam's litany came to an end as the nurse pushed through the door with the medications.

"Good morning, Sam. Wake up, Arthur! It's time for your pills. It's a special day, Sam. Do you remember what day it is?"

"I don't know. Tuesday, maybe?"

"No, Saturday. You're going to have a lot of company today. This is your birthday, Sam. Do you remember how old you are today?"

"I guess I'd be about 103."

"That's right. One hundred and three years old. Everyone is coming for your birthday party today. All of your grandchildren and great-grandchildren, and I've heard you even have a couple of great-great-grandsons."

"I think they even named one of them after me."

"Well, April will be in in another hour or so to get you your breakfast and bath. When you're all dressed and ready we'll take some pictures with all of your friends. Happy Birthday, Sam!"

One hundred and three. As he swallowed his pills, Sam's mind drifted back to the light-hearted days of his youth, when he and his friends used to say things like, "I'll never under-stand that if I live to be a hundred." Things don't really change, Sam thought. I've lived to be more than a hundred, and there are so many things I still don't understand. "Do not cast me off in the time of old age." "Weeping may linger with the night, but joy comes in the morning." Sam sighed and lay back to watch and wait.

———————————

Story Questions

1. Do you think Sam was miserable living in the nursing home? Support your answer with an example from the story.

2. What were the things Sam found it most difficult to live without?

3. Have you ever had a relative in a nursing home? What was most difficult for that person about being there?

4. What was Sam's greatest comfort in his daily life? What does that say to us as Christians?

5. Do you expect to live in a nursing home when you are old? What would be the pluses? The minuses?

Digging Into The Text

*Rescue me, O my God, from the hand of the wicked,
from the grasp of the unjust and cruel. For you, O Lord,
are my hope, my trust, O Lord, from my youth. Upon
you I have leaned from my birth; it was you who took
me from my mother's womb. My praise is continually
of you.*

*I have been like a portent to many, but you are my strong
refuge. My mouth is filled with your praise, and with your
glory all day long. Do not cast me off in the time of old
age; do not forsake me when my strength is spent.*

*O God, from my youth you have taught me, and I still
proclaim your wondrous deeds. So even to old age and
gray hairs, O God, do not forsake me, until I proclaim
your might to all the generations to come. Your power
and your righteousness, O God, reach the high heavens.*
                                        Psalm 71:4-9, 17-19

An elderly man appeals to God for help in this prayer/song
which was written to be sung in the temple in Jerusalem. There
is no doubt that the author is very old and that he suffers from
the infirmities that have afflicted the elderly in every age. He
expresses fear that he will be abandoned, cast off, forsaken:
that he will be put to shame. He is afraid of his enemies, of
those who are wicked, unjust and cruel. And because he is too
feeble to protect himself, he pleads with God for refuge,
deliverance, help: to be saved not forsaken, to be rescued. "Do
not forsake me" is repeated twice. There is a tone of despera-
tion in this psalm. The words "rescue" and "refuge" are
repeated three times.

Imagine a chorus of elderly women and men singing this
ancient Jerusalem temple hymn in one of our modern
cathedrals or in the corridor of a local nursing home. See the
gray heads lined up row upon row, some in wheelchairs, others
strapped into their beds, all lifting up their voices to the creator, pleading:

Do not cast me off in the time of old age; do not forsake
me when my strength is spent (v. 9). So even to old age
and gray hairs, O God, do not forsake me . . . (v. 18).

Thousands of elderly Americans who are abandoned by
their families and their churches every year sing their own ver-
sions of this psalm. Donna Swanson's poem "Minnie Remembers" conveys the plaintive spirit of the psalmist's words:

How long has it been since someone touched me?
Twenty years?
Twenty years I've been a widow.
Respected.
Smiled at.
But never touched.
Never held close to another body.
Never held so close and warm that the loneliness
was blotted out.

Why didn't we raise the kids to be
silly and affectionate
as well as dignified and proper?
You see, they do their duty.
They drive up in their fine cars,
The come to my room to pay their respects.
They chatter brightly and reminisce
But they don't touch me.

They call me "Mom" or "Mother" or "Grandma."
Never Minnie
My mother called me Minnie
And my friends.

Hank called me Minnie, too.
But they're gone.
And so is Minnie.
Only Grandma is here.
And God! She's lonely!

The odds of living to be as old as Minnie, and perhaps as
lonely, are increasing every day. Stephen Sapp reports in his

book, *Light on a Gray Area: American Public Policy on Aging,* "Currently, over 80 percent of Americans live from birth to age 70, up from 20 percent in 1900" (39). More significantly, he says:

> ... those 85 and older ... termed by demographers the "oldest old" has grown from a few hundred thousand in 1900 to over 3 million today and is projected to number between 15 and 20 million by 2050. Those 85 and over, who are 10 percent of the older population today, will make up as much as 30 percent of the elderly by the middle of the next century ... Not surprisingly, the number of people over 100 will rise significantly as well, from about 3,000 thirty years ago to 50,000 today, and to well over 100,000 by the turn of the century (41).

Sapp indicates that this impending increase of numbers of the "oldest old" will have other far-reaching effects:

> These ... numbers are especially noteworthy because they contain major implications for provision of care. Carl Eisdorfer, an internationally recognized geriatric psychiatrist and one of the founders of the organization now known as the Alzheimer's Association, estimates the need for care doubles with every five years of age over 65 ... 23 percent of the entire noninstitutionalized population 65 and over have difficulty with "personal care activities" such as eating, dressing and bathing (41).

Living to a "ripe old age" is not necessarily a blessing. Margaret Skeete, who was listed in the *Guinness Book of World Records* as the oldest living American until her death in May of 1994 at the age of 115, professed not to be impressed by her longevity. "I guess that's something, but it doesn't buy me anything," she said on her 115th birthday. Mrs. Skeete had been a widow for 41 years and was preceded in death by 2 of her 3 children. She was living with her daughter at the time of her death (Associated Press, 2).

Mrs. Skeete was fortunate to have a child who was willing and able to take her in. Like Sam in Jo's touching story, "If I Live To Be A Hundred," she could have been living unhappily in a nursing home for years and years. And worse yet, she could have become one of 70,000 elderly parents who are abandoned every year in the United States by family members who are unwilling or unable to care for them. "Granny dumping," as this abandonment is now known, was unheard of 15 years ago, according to John Meyers, a spokesman for the American Association of Retired Persons. "Not a day goes by when a hospital emergency room somewhere in America doesn't have a case where some elderly person is abandoned, usually by the children" (Egan, A1).

The most celebrated case of "granny dumping" was reported in March of 1992, after John Kingery, an 82-year-old Alzheimer's victim from Portland, Oregon, was abandoned by his daughter at an Idaho dog racing track. Oregon was the first state in the nation to arrange exemptions from the Medicaid laws to allow Medicaid to pay for adult care at home or with a foster family, thereby easing financial burdens on the family, but it hasn't prevented parent dumping. Ironically, there are gaps in the law that do not protect the elderly from such abandonment. In Idaho, where Mr. Kingery was found, it is illegal to abandon a dog or a child, but not an elderly person. In Oregon such an offense is punishable by up to a year in jail. Meyers says such abandonments are indicative of the terrible balancing act care-givers are stuck with, and it will only become worse. The number of people over age 65 is expected to reach 60 million by the year 2030, and those who suffer from Alzheimer's could reach 12 million by the year 2020 (A9).

A double irony of John Kingery's case was reported by Ellen Goodman in her April 12, 1992, syndicated column. She related the story of Kingery's daughter Nancy, one of five children from a previous marriage, who had not been in contact with her father for the 28 years since he divorced their mother and remarried. When she recognized him from pictures accompanying the stories of his abandonment, she joyfully arranged to visit him in his nursing home. In Goodman's words:

> *The pathos in their nursing home reunion is hard to overstate. A 55-year-old woman tearfully and gratefully greeting an 82-year-old father who could no longer recognize her. "I didn't have a Dad all those years," she said. "Now I have one." One who does not know his own name. Or hers. But a father all the same.*
>
> *What a mix of family dramas in this sad tale. Granny dumping and kiddie dumping. Children who abandon their parents and parents who abandon their children. But what my ear picked up in Nancy Myatt's words was the simple, endless hunger of a child of any age for a father who disappeared.*

Concern and caring for one's parents is a frequent biblical theme. One of the last things Jesus did on the cross before he died was to see that his mother was cared for. He said to her, pointing to John, "Woman, behold your son!" Then he said to the disciple, "Behold your mother!" And from that hour the disciple took her to his own home (John 19:26-27).

Honoring the old was so important in preserving the integrity of the family, and thus the whole fabric of society, that it was included as one of the Ten Commandments. Most of us have been familiar with these words since our training in Sunday school. It is a verse teachers often use to teach children to be obedient to their parents. However, this fifth commandment was not given for the benefit of Hebrew children. To a child growing up in a Jewish family this commandment would have been as superfluous as "thou must breathe" or "thou must eat." Like the other nine commandments, it is directed toward adult citizens. It warns them not to adopt the heathen practice of abandoning old people to the wild animals when they are ill or no longer economically useful. Some of the pagan nations of that time had a custom of leaving old people out in the wilderness to die when they were no longer able to care for themselves. Old people in Jewish society play an important role in handing down traditions and teaching its laws. The fifth commandment left no doubt about the value of the aged in the new nation God would establish for Israel in the promised land (Buttrick, 985).

On a deeper level the fifth commandment says that God was giving the promised land to the old as well as the young, and that the young could not expect to have a good life there in the future unless the old had a good life in the present. The way they treated their aged parents was the way they could expect to be treated by their children when they grew old.

This is just as true for us today. Many people dread retirement and fear old age because they have witnessed the unhappiness of some of their older relatives and friends. Deep down we fear that, like them, we may end our days with nothing meaningful to do, no money, no one who cares for us, and nowhere to live but a nursing home. We fear growing old because, as a society, we have not provided sufficiently for the needs of the elderly.

In recent years there have been advances in this area, but while the elderly may have many more benefits than they have ever had before in the form of social security, medicare, low-rent housing, advanced medical technology and more modern nursing care facilities, they have lost something much more important than financial security. That is a significant role in society and the respect due old age. Many elderly people are given no useful function, and so have no purpose, no reason for being. They find meaning only in memories of times past, and they long for the day when death will relieve them of the emptiness of old age without honor.

Sharon Curtin recognized this problem more than 20 years ago, when she wrote in her book *Nobody Ever Died of Old Age:*

> *Traditional roles for the aged have vanished. There are no quiet, warm spaces by the fireplace to sit and watch your grandchildren play, no cracker barrels to sit upon and speak of times past . . . We live in a culture which*

endorses what has been called human obsolescence. To the junk heap, the nursing home, the retirement village, the last resort ... There is no security in old age (17).

Ms. Curtin is right. And if there is no security in old age, there is no security at any age. She included the following story as a perfect example:

> *There is an old American folktale about a wooden bowl. It seems that Grandmother, with her trembling hands, was guilty of occasionally breaking a dish. Her daughter angrily gave her a wooden bowl and told her that she must eat out of it from now on. The young granddaughter, observing this, asked her mother why Grandmother must eat from a wooden bowl when the rest of the family was given china plates. "Because she is old," answered the mother. The child thought for a moment and then told her mother, "You must save the wooden bowl when Grandma dies." Her mother asked why, and the child replied, "For when you are old" (196-197).*

Along with the aging of the Baby Boom generation has come an increased push toward maintaining a youthful appearance, exercising, eating sensibly, and prolonging quality life for as long as possible. Charles Inlander and Marie Hodge have written a book for the mindset of the '90s titled *100 Ways to Live to 100*, in which they assert, "The single most important step you can take to prolong your life, next to quitting smoking, may be reducing saturated fat and cholesterol in your diet." Why, when society has so little time and accommodation for the elderly, would we *try* to live to such an age? The answer has to do with the alternative. Americans are afraid to die. At the same time, we fear what growing old will do to our minds, our bodies, our lives, and so we strive while we are in middle-age to change the way society has been to a more acceptable, more comfortable pattern for our own futures.

I am 43 years old. If I live to be a hundred, I will have 57 more years of life on this earth. I wonder what the quality of those years might be for me. Like the psalmist, I fear abandonment. I take comfort in the fact that I have two wonderful children who love me, but I know there is no guarantee they will live as long as I do, or that they will be in a position to care for me physically or emotionally when I am no longer able to care for myself.

Last night I was called to visit a 90-year-old woman who is dying. She lives in a very comfortable nursing home operated by my denomination. The staff seemed pleasant and caring. Her roommate was also clearly a friend and very much interested in her welfare. As I was leaving, I passed an elderly man in the lobby visiting with his son. Will I be so fortunate in my declining years? I know other older persons who have no surviving family or friends who live in foul-smelling, dingy nursing homes with uncaring staff. The prayer of the psalmist is heard daily in such places, "Do not forsake me . . . ."

My grandmother, Leona Long, was born December 2, 1887. She was 105 years old when she died in January of 1993. She stood less than five feet tall and weighed less than a hundred pounds all her life, and she was one of the strongest persons I have ever known. Grandma was the granddaughter of Irish immigrants who left their homeland during the potato famine of 1859 and settled in Richland County, Wisconsin. Her grandfather, Edward John Long, was a graduate of the University of Dublin and an ordained minister. He fought in the American Civil War with four of his brothers. Grandma loved to tell us the stories she had learned at her grandfather's knee: how he was wounded in the eye and imprisoned at Andersonville. Sometimes when I asked she would tell about the hardships of her own life: about my uncle Robert who died at the age of four, and my aunt Florence who died on Christmas Eve at the age of three. My grandfather was killed in an auto accident in the 34th year of their marriage. Grandma was a widow for 47 years. Her motto was "keep on keeping on."

If you asked Grandma the secret of her longevity, she would have told you it was horehound candy. She said it kept her regular. And she believed that she had had a guardian angel since a close call when she was four years old. She was fond of telling how she went to fetch a pail of water and saw a rattlesnake ahead of her on the path. She was about to step over it when she felt something holding her back, and it held her until the snake had passed on its way.

Grandma lived the last 11 years of her life in a nursing home. She told us often how frustrating it was to be old. She said, "I remember things from years ago, but I can't remember what happened yesterday." I asked her once if she had ever expected to live to be 100. "Oh, no!" she said. She was amazed to find herself still living after all those years, and more than a little aggravated with God. Again and again she would say, "Oh, why am I still here? I'm as old as the hills. What could God possibly have for me to do?" We always put our arms around her and told her we loved her and that for our own selfish reasons, we were glad she was still with us. But we understood what she was saying, and in our hearts we prayed with her the prayer of the psalmist, "Do not cast me off in the time of old age; do not forsake me when my strength is spent."

Digging Into The Text Questions

1. Do you know anyone who is over 100 years old? If so, describe the quality of his/her life.

2. Subtract your current age from 100. How many years do you have left to live if you live to be 100? Would you like to live that long?

3. Did your parents care for your aging grandparents? Did your grandparents go to live in a nursing home? Discuss how either or both of these options worked. What are the benefits and disadvantages?

4. Are you now caring for, or do you expect to have to care for, your own aging parents? What difficulties exist? What difficulties do you foresee?

5. Do you expect your children to be responsible for your care when you no longer can be? Would you want to live with them?

6. List some changes you would like to see in government responsibility toward the aged, in programs for the aged, or in healthcare for the aged.

Works Cited

Associated Press. "Oldest American Dies at 115." *The Kenosha News.* 8, May 1994: 2.

Buttrick, George Arthur, Ed. *The Interpreters Bible.* Nashville: Abingdon Press, 1952, vol. 1: 985.

Curtin, Sharon R. *Nobody Ever Died of Old Age.* Boston: Little, Brown & Co., 1972.

Egan, Timothy. special to *The New York Times.* 26, Mar. 1992: A1 +.

Goodman, Ellen. "Daughter Ditches Dad, But Another Finds Him." *The Kenosha News.* 12, Apr. 1992.

The Holy Bible, New Revised Standard Version.

Islander, Charles and Marie Hodge. *100 Ways to Live to 100.* New York: Wing Books, 1992.

Sapp, Stephen. *Light on a Gray Area: American Public Policy on Aging.* Nashville: Abingdon Press, 1992.

Swanson, Donna. "Minnie Remembers."